REACHING ADOLESCENTS:

INTERDATING, INTERMARRIAGE, AND JEWISH IDENTITY

A PROGRAM GUIDE

Commission on Reform Jewish Outreach of the
Union of American Hebrew Congregations and the
Central Conference of American Rabbis

Copyright © 1990, Union of American Hebrew Congregations
Manufactured in the United States of America
1 2 3 4 5 6 7 8 9

This Program Guide is dedicated to
DAVID BELIN
first Chairman, UAHC/CCAR Commission on Reform Jewish Outreach
whose love of the Jewish people and concern for Jewish
survival have inspired the work of Outreach

Judaism is like a flower
One among millions
I never noticed how bright its colors
or its uniqueness
Until I saw the hand
reach down to pick it
I grabbed that hand
and tried my best
To keep its colors
brighter than ever.

Heather Blaine, age 16
Winchester, MA
Summer, 1989
Academy II, Kutz Camp

This poem was written as part of a 15 session discussion program on exploring Jewish identity.

Table of Contents

	Page
Acknowledgments	1
Section One:	
Introduction	5
Workshop: Understanding Adolescence	7
Part I: A Journey Back	8
Part II: A Brief Overview of Adolescence; Programming Tips	12
Section Two:	
Part I: Warm-up Exercises	21
Part II: Programs on Interdating and Intermarriage	29
Part III: Reform Jewish Identity and Values Clarification	51
Part IV: Programs Using Historical Perspectives and Text Studies	85
Appendices:	
1: Program Planning Worksheet	119
2: Program Evaluation Worksheet	121
3: Program Evaluation Form	123
4: What Is Outreach?	125
5: Suggested Reading	131
6: Regional Outreach Coordinators	133

Acknowledgements

UAHC - CCAR Commission on Reform Jewish Outreach

Melvin Merians, *Chairman*
Rabbi Leslie Gutterman, *Co-Chairman*
Lydia Kukoff, *Director and Executive Editor*
Rabbi Nina J. Mizrahi, *Associate Director and Editor*
Sherri Alper, *Consultant for Special Programming*
Dru Greenwood, *Coordinator, Task Force on the Unaffiliated*

Regional Outreach Staff

Canadian Council, Jessie Caryll
Great Lakes Council/Chicago Federation, Mimi Dunitz
Mid-Atlantic Council, Elizabeth Farquhar
Midwest Council, Marsha Luhrs
New Jersey/West Hudson Valley Council, Kathryn Kahn
New York Federation of Reform Synagogues, Ellyn Geller
Northeast Council, Paula Brody
Northeast Lakes Council, Nancy Gad-Harf
Northern California Council/Pacific Northwest Council, Lisa Cohen Bennett
Pacific Southwest Council, Arlene Chernow
Pennsylvania Council/Philadelphia Federation, Linda Steigman
Southeast Council/South Florida Federation, Rabbi Rachel Hertzman
Southwest Council, Debby Stein

Administrative Staff: Muriel Finn, Gail Sussnow
Cover Design: Rayleen Buys, Helayne Friedland

* * *

We express special gratitude to:

SHERRI ALPER, A.C.S.W., whose expertise in creating programs has enriched this program guide immeasurably

LISA COHEN BENNETT, Ph.D., whose work inspired this publication and who helped us to connect with our own adolescence and to reach out more sensitively and effectively to our young people

ELLYN GELLER, whose gift for working with teenagers has provided us with many valuable insights into Jewish identity development

SECTION ONE

UNDERSTANDING ADOLESCENCE

REACHING ADOLESCENTS: INTERDATING, INTERMARRIAGE, AND JEWISH IDENTITY

Introduction

The first decade of Outreach has taught us one particularly valuable lesson: Outreach is not only about intermarriage and conversion. <u>It is about being Jewish</u>. Outreach enables us to look inward at who we are as Jews and outward toward our changing community. Awareness of each enriches the other.

The work of the UAHC/CCAR Commission on Reform Jewish Outreach during the past decade has had profound implications for the entire Jewish community, illuminating the path toward authentic and meaningful Reform Jewish identity. Our goals for the next ten years of Outreach are to understand these implications and to develop programs which further strengthen our Jewish identity.

This program guide represents a first step in our Inreach efforts. Its purpose is to help young people address issues relating to interdating, intermarriage and Jewish identity.

In working with young people we have learned that one cannot talk about interdating and intermarriage without exploring personal Jewish identity. By encouraging adolescents to look seriously at their own Jewish identity, we increase the likelihood that they will be advocates for Judaism in their lives.

This packet provides resources and programming ideas for pre-teens through college-age youth on issues of interdating, intermarriage, and Jewish identity.

<u>Section I</u> provides background material on adolescence. Presented as a workshop, this portion is best facilitated by a mental health professional with expertise in child and adolescent development. If such a person is not available, you will still find the exercises valuable and you should not hesitate to try them.

<u>Section II</u> outlines programs that have been used successfully with teenagers. The section is divided into four parts:

1. "Warm-up Exercises"
2. "Programs on Interdating and Intermarriage"
3. "Reform Jewish Identity and Values Clarification"
4. "Programs using Historical Perspectives and Text Studies"

All the information you need to ensure that your program is a success is included.

The <u>Appendices</u> contain useful background and resource material.

This packet has been published as an experimental edition. We want to hear about the programs that work best for you. Program ideas, insights, comments, and concerns should be addressed to the UAHC/CCAR Commission on Reform Jewish Outreach, 838 Fifth Avenue, New York, N.Y. 10021. Your regional Outreach coordinator, whose name and telephone number can be found in <u>Appendix 6</u>, can provide invaluable assistance to you in any area of program planning.

Our tradition tells a tale about two men who were wandering in the woods when they came upon one another. "Do you know the way out of the woods?" asked one. "No, I cannot tell you how to go. But perhaps if we show one another the paths we have tried, then we can find the way together."

Let us hear from you!

WORKSHOP: UNDERSTANDING ADOLESCENTS

The following workshop is intended to sensitize adults to the experience of adolescence. Participants may include teachers, rabbis, religious school and youth group committee members, and youth group advisors. It is most effectively led by a mental health professional with expertise in child and adolescent development, but the exercises will be useful background regardless of the facilitator chosen.

The entire workshop requires a total of approximately two hours, or one hour for each part. Part I includes a guided fantasy whose purpose is to help participants remember their own teenage years. Part II draws on the experience of participants in order to consider adolescent development from a broader perspective.

Before beginning, you will need the following materials: a blackboard or large pad, chalk or felt-tipped pens, and photocopies of appropriate exercises included in this packet for each participant.

PART I: A JOURNEY BACK

Instructions for the Facilitator:
Begin by asking for a volunteer to read aloud the following excerpt from a presentation delivered to youth group advisors by Dr. Seymour Siegler (excerpted from: "The Adolescent and the Advisor," by Dr. Seymour Siegler. Reprinted with permission. The phrases within the parentheses were added by Lisa Cohen Bennett):

> Understanding the adolescent is the perennial concern of parents, teachers, youth workers, and, yes, of adolescents themselves. Does understanding really come so hard? It's just that those of us who work with adolescents sometimes succumb to one or more of three basic errors in understanding our young charges:
>
> (1) we <u>over-generalize</u> about classic teenage problems;
>
> (2) we are inclined to <u>forget our own</u> adolescent adjustment problems (a blessing that creeping old age bestows upon us); and
>
> (3) we tend toward myopia about these problems of adjustment that are <u>unique</u> to the current generation of adolescents.
>
> First, over-generalization leaves us with a rather short catalog of cliches and catch-phrases to which we frequently nod vigorous assent when we come together to commiserate. You know the phrases: "identity crisis," "peer pressure," "asserting oneself," "part adult and part child," "developing a self-concept." This kind of idea exchange tends to paint a somewhat one-dimensional and stereotypical picture of the gangling, erratic, irresponsible organism preoccupied with hair and skin and talking back to Mom and Dad. Are we ever caught considering the aspirations of teenagers; their social conscience; their sexuality; their attitudes toward love and faith and learning; and, their fears about death and career and disease and decision and God and loneliness?
>
> Secondly, when we reflect upon our own adolescent years, what are the dimensions of our memories? Often, they constitute only that brief encyclopedia of interesting stories we carry with us to chuckle over for the rest of our lives. Do we remember the sorrows; the loneliness; the indecision? And what about the private thoughts we had about our parents, our friends, members of the opposite (or same) sex? Do we carry any unresolved pain from that time? What did we laugh about and cry about privately and secretly? No need for psychoanalysis here; just a gentle reminder that life during the high school years was full of dimensions of experience way beyond what we filter out and choose to recall.
>
> Finally, it can be noted that we may be many more generations removed from the teenage charges we work with than we imagine.

We can no longer measure generations in terms of 10 or 20 year segments. Take a hard look at what your adolescents are talking and worrying about today. Check to see if you had a similar array of problems. If you did not then a generation or more has gone by. You might be 2,3,4, or 20 years away from them in time, yet those concerns impact on growing up today. There is certainly your legacy of concerns and mine; but these days the list not only is cumulative but gets longer faster, e.g. effects on the family of the economic crunch; the pornography explosion; the decline of social protest; the drug culture; the VD (and AIDS) epidemic; the knowledge and technology explosion; the new morality; and whatever the latest series of jolts are to the values of preceding generations.

Not trapping ourselves in these errors is the first step in understanding the adolescent. There is no typical adolescent, just as there is no typical Jew.

Discussion Questions:
Ask the group for their reactions, using the following discussion questions as a guide:

1. What are the "classic teenage problems" to which the author is referring? Why are these stereotypes?

2. What are the particular problems of teens in our community?

3. What kinds of adolescent behavior are particularly difficult for you in your role as teacher/advisor/rabbi etc.? How do you react to it?

4. Describe an "ideal" adolescent. Does s/he exist in reality? Do your expectations take into consideration the kinds of problems to which Siegler refers?

Conclude the discussion by noting that general concerns of adolescents include the following:

> Do my peers like me?
> Am I attractive?
> What will I be when I grow up?
> How can I become independent?
> Should I try cigarettes/alcohol/sex/drugs?

In addition to the general concerns most teenager share, individual family, educational, class,religious, and socioeconomic concerns abound. While it is easy to generalize about developmental characteristics, it is important to remember that in many respects, each teenager is different.

Guided Fantasy:
The purpose of the next part of this workshop is to help participants recall their own teenage years in order to sensitize them to the experience of adolescents. Give them a moment to stand up and stretch before settling back into their chairs in the most comfortable position possible. Explain that the exercise is a guided fantasy whose objective is to help them remember their own adolescence.

You may use the following narrative as a guide, substituting your own words where desired. Be sure to soften your voice and read slowly.

"Close your eyes and find a comfortable position in the chair. It is important to be as relaxed as possible for our journey back in time. Be aware of any parts of your body that are tense, and make a conscious effort to relax those muscles. Take a few breaths, and notice how good it feels just to sit quietly. Think about your facial muscles, and let them relax, too.

"I want you to think about a photograph taken of yourself when you were in junior high school. Perhaps it is a school picture. Maybe it's a snapshot in your photograph album. Maybe it's a picture that exists nowhere except in your mind. Notice what you're wearing...how your hair looks...the expression on your face...

"What do you remember about being a young teenager? What happy memories are tucked away with those years? Perhaps you're remembering leaving your elementary school to be with the older kids...your Bar or Bat Mitzvah...your friends. As you recall being 12...13...14..., visualize the places and the faces around you.... You may find some special memories of those summers.... Remember just what it felt like to be growing up so quickly during those years...with _your_ friends.... What kinds of things did you worry about then?...

"Now I'd like you to move forward in time...you're entering high school. Remember how you looked when you were 15... 16... 17... 18.... Remember what the building looked like, the noise of the hallways between classes, the teachers you saw every day, your friends. What did you care about during those years? What do you remember? A special friend? School? Camp? Driving? Confirmation? Perhaps you remember the experience of being in love.... Find some pictures for the scrapbook in your mind: pictures of you, pictures of your friends, pictures of your family.... Some of the pictures will be happy ones, and some -- even today -- might be sad.

"Before we finish, remember that this is just a journey. You're looking at memories that are special only to you. You might recall some of them with a smile, some with sadness. Some of them you will want to share...others may be private.... They are all a part of the person you have become.

"The pages of an imaginary calendar are flipping forward quickly through the years, bringing you, finally, to your current age...to your life in the present. When you are ready to return to this room, open your eyes slowly. Your journey is complete."

The facilitator asks participants about their reactions to the guided fantasy. As they were remembering, did they feel far removed from the experiences and feelings? Were they surprised by any of their memories or reactions?

Have the following chart already written on the blackboard or a large pad:

Self	Important People	Support People	Parents	Other Adults

Ask the group to begin by thinking of words that best describe them as a teenager. List the adjectives that participants use underneath the "Self" column on the board. Proceed with each of the other columns, using the following questions as a guide: Who were the most important people in your life? (positive and negative). Where did you get your support? What adjectives would you use to describe your parents? How would you describe your relationship with them? How did you feel about other adults?

Ask participants to look at the chart you have just made. While each of them chose words that applied to them individually in remembering their adolescence, the chart begins to provide a broad description of what it's like to be a teenager. Many of the words used paint a picture of the young people with whom they work.

Ask the group to consider all the columns as a whole. Comment on the number of entries, and the animated discussion of important adults in their lives as adolescents. Adults played very important roles during that period in their lives. While many people assume that teenagers don't/won't listen to adults, it's very clear that they do. Don't underestimate the power of even a brief encounter with a teenager!

Ask the group if they have any final comments before moving on to the next portion of the workshop, a brief lecture and discussion of adolescent development.

****

PART II: A BRIEF OVERVIEW OF ADOLESCENCE; PROGRAMMING TIPS

Adolescence:
In order to enable participants to generalize from their own experiences as teenagers, the facilitator provides a brief overview of adolescent development and leads a discussion of issues as they arise. The following suggestions will maximize the usefulness of this part of the workshop:

1. Do not permit lengthy discussion at this point of the participants' own experiences as adolescents. The goal now is to move from personal issues to a broader understanding.

2. Be sure to connect the theoretical with the experiences of participants in working with teenagers. Ask for specific examples of the behaviors described.

3. In discussing adolescent development, ask participants which areas present special difficulty to them in their work. Encourage self-awareness, and reassure participants that everyone who works with teens at times finds their behavior a challenge.

4. Note that while some of this material may be a review, its understanding is crucial to successful program development.

The facilitator begins by making the following points:

1. Adolescents experience the most rapid and varied changes in their development since infancy. The five generally acknowledged areas of growth are: physical, emotional, social, moral, intellectual. (Write these categories on the board as column headings).

2. Ask the group to give examples of _physical_ changes, and write them under the appropriate column. Examples include: sexual maturity, including breast development and the onset of menses in girls and the growth of facial and body hair and sexual maturity in boys; changes in appearance, including rapid growth and possible onset of teenage acne; physical awkwardness, etc. If your group has difficulty discussing various aspects of sexual maturity, you may choose to remark on how difficult a subject it is to discuss, even for mature adults. Imagine (or remember) how difficult it is for teens!

3. Ask for examples of <u>emotional</u> development and write them on the board. Examples include: Frequent moodiness; the development of mature empathy; introspection and concern with "Who am I?"; concerns related to loneliness and isolation; increasing emotional distance from the family and intense relationships with peers of both sexes; occasional withdrawal, etc.

4. Ask for examples of <u>social</u> development. Participants will probably include involvement with peers; conformity vs. individuality; concern with social values and "causes"; inconsistency in relationship with adults; struggles with authority, etc.

5. What are some examples of <u>moral</u> development? Note that it is difficult to separate moral, social, and emotional development, since the three are closely linked. Examples of moral development include increasing ability to make appropriate judgments about right and wrong; concern for social justice; concern with both individual moral choices and ethical behavior in general, etc. The adolescent's concern with morality provides a very natural point of entry for the discussion of many religious issues.

6. Finally, significant growth in <u>intellectual</u> development occurs during the teenage years. Ask the group for examples, which may include the following: increased ability to think abstractly; passion for discussion and debate; increased capacity for introspection, etc.

Remind participants that not all of the examples given apply to all teenagers. Some are more characteristic of the early teenage years while others occur later. It is also important to note that individual differences, family and social environment all play a role in the extent to which particular teens experience the changes described. While generalizing helps us to understand the developmental processes of adolescence, it is important to remember that we are working with individuals.

Finally, distribute copies of the following handout to participants, briefly reviewing the categories of development and focusing on suggested adult responses.

Responding to Adolescents:
Tips for Group Leaders

* **Early Adolescence** (Ages 12-15)

The developmental task of early adolescence is to begin to discover personal identity, based upon: 1) the integration of family, religious and societal values; 2) the understanding of the self in relation to peers and adults; 3) relating differently to those of the opposite sex; and 4) projecting self-concept into the future.

Normal Characteristics of Young Teens	Suggestions for Adult Response
* Changes in <u>physical</u> appearance as the body matures. Self-consciousness, restlessness, frequent hunger.	* Compliment appearance. Respect and tolerate awkwardness. Provide healthy snacks.
* <u>Intellectual</u> development is often reflected in teenagers' passion for discussion, debate, and frequent role as devil's advocate; Intellectual development and the ability to think abstractly increase along with the capacity for introspection; Commitment to ideals becomes stronger.	* Discuss rather than lecture. Don't underestimate teens' intellectual abilities, and provide <u>choice</u> everywhere possible for them to pursue individual interests. Relate all material to the individual. ("What does all this mean for us?") Explore values.
* <u>Social</u> development in early adolescence is most often characterized by increased independence from parents; intense relationships with peers of same sex; frequent impatience with anyone younger; continual comparisons of self to peers; and occasional rude behavior toward adult authority.	* Plan educational programs to take into account interest in relating primarily to peers. Acknowledge the need to feel connected to others (and note that this continues, with varying intensity, throughout the life span). Understand the basis of occasional inappropriate behavior toward adult authority, but set appropriate limits and provide feedback.

* <u>Moral</u> development between
  ages 12 and 15 is reflected
  in teenagers' need to consider
  right and wrong on the basis
  of internalized personal values
  rather than moral dictums.
  Increased concern for the
  disenfranchised and oppressed.

* Communicate respect
  for the teenager as an
  individual with passionate
  feelings about justice and
  fair play. Avoid moralizing
  lectures in favor of
  discussion about the
  foundation for morality and
  how perspectives may have
  evolved. Underline the
  need to make personal
  decisions within a social
  and religious context.

* For young adolescents, common
  <u>emotional</u> characteristics
  may include moodiness, anxiety,
  emotional highs and lows,
  and withdrawal, all <u>within
  normal limits.</u>

* Communicate respect for
  feelings. Model the
  <u>expression</u> of emotion.
  Encourage cooperation
  and inclusion, but do
  not pressure an occasionally
  moody or withdrawn teenager
  to participate. Express
  concern about emotional
  behavior that appears to
  go beyond normal limits
  and follow up
  appropriately.

* <u>Late Adolescence</u> (Ages 16-19)

The developmental task of late adolescence is to complete the
evolution of a relatively mature personal identity, based upon:
1) the integration of family, religion, and societal values;
2) an understanding of the self in relation to peers and adults;
3) increasing confidence in relating to the opposite sex; and
4) increased clarity regarding projecting the self into the
future (choices regarding higher education, vocational options,
etc.)

<u>Normal Characteristics</u>

<u>Suggestions for Adult Response</u>

* <u>Physical</u> development is
  completed. Some level of
  sexual activity is likely.

* Compliment appearance and
  physical maturity.
  Acknowledge sexuality as a
  normal part of maturity. Relate
  sexuality to socio-religious
  context. Provide accurate
  information about sexuality.

* <u>Mental</u> development is reflected in concerns regarding: "measuring up" in relation to peers; educational and vocational choices; and an evolving sense of personal learning style and preferences.

* Highlight talents. Acknowledge academic pressure by educational institutions and parents. <u>Ask</u> how they learn best and for their perspectives on their secular and religious education to date.

* <u>Social</u> relationships with same sex peers remain active, while romantic relationships with opposite sex may take on new intensity. Desire to function as independent adults without parental involvement. New readiness to accept non-parental adult mentors as role models.

* Applaud and encourage responsible independence. Discuss romantic relationships and realistic expectations about dating and marriage. Respect privacy.

* <u>Moral</u> development in late adolescence may be characterized by expressions of confusion, helplessness, and anger about injustice. Need to see a tangible connection between values and action.

* Discuss ethical and moral dilemmas faced by teens through an understanding of the socio/religious context. Discuss discrepancies between "what is" and "what might be." Provide opportunity for social action.

* During late adolescence, common <u>emotional</u> characteristics include: increased desire for independence (and concurrent fears about its meaning and management); occasional moodiness and a tendency to be self-absorbed; and some anxiety about the future.

* Expect inconsistent behavior. Provide increased autonomy, but set appropriate limits. Acknowledge ambivalence about separation.

Finally, by letting adolescents know that:

   *you understand what it's like to be an adolescent

   *you will not judge them (only their behavior)

   *you are available to listen

   *you remember what it was like

you will go a long way in gaining their trust and helping them grow.

Programming Tips:

In this section you will find all the information you need to plan successful programs for teenagers. Included in this section are:

I. An introduction to successful programming, and

II. Complete directions for programs in each of the following areas:

> Warm-up Exercises
>
> Programs on Interdating and Intermarriage
>
> Programs on Reform Jewish Identity and Values Clarification
>
> Historical Perspectives and Text Studies

The Outreach Component:

Questions raised by Jewish parents and professionals about interdating and intermarriage reflect deeper concerns about the strength of Jewish identity of our adolescents. While it may be tempting to offer a single program specifically about interdating and intermarriage, experience suggests that a carefully planned series which includes programming from each of the categories outlined above will encourage teenagers to grapple effectively with the issues and will be less likely to be viewed as an attempt to control behavior and limit choices.

Programs should encourage participants to explore their Jewish identity and to understand how deeply it influences choices they make in their lives. It is important that programs maintain a balance between values clarification exercises, which respond to the needs of individuals in the group, and substantive material on Judaism and Jewish identity. Experience in programming during the first decade of Outreach has strengthened our belief that Outreach is not about conversion and intermarriage: it is about being Jewish.

Facilitators should be familiar with Outreach and its work before undertaking any of these programs. A brief description can be found in <u>Appendix 4</u>. It is helpful to share with teenagers our pride in our movement's courage to grapple with what, in other arenas, is still often discussed in whispers.

Facilitators must also take care to demonstrate sensitivity to the backgrounds of all participants. There may be teens whose parents are intermarried, who may have one or both parents who are Jews by Choice, or who come from blended families with step-parents and step-siblings who are not Jewish.

PLANNING A SUCCESSFUL PROGRAM

Before Beginning:
Working with adolescents requires the ability to think on your feet. Teenagers will challenge your assumptions, play devil's advocate, and debate the issues that arise. Before beginning any program, be certain that you have fully considered the following areas which are bound to arise in discussion:

Interdating:
"Why not date a non-Jew? I'm not going to marry one!"

"If I only dated Jews I'd be doomed to stay home forever."

Intermarriage:
"My parents are intermarried, and they're doing fine."

"All this talk about intermarriage just divides people. I think we need to look at what we have in common and how we can unite people."

Jewish Identity:
"Why should I want to stay Jewish?"

"We all believe in the same God. That's all that matters."

Being Jewish in a Christian World:
"I don't want to always be different. I want to be like everybody else."

"I don't believe that Jews are necessarily better than everyone else. My Christian friends have better values than many Jews I know."

There are no "correct" responses to these issues. Remember that adolescents need to be heard, even when we disagree with their point of view.

It is important for facilitators not to give the impression that they have all the answers. Outreach began as a resolution to use our most creative selves to grapple with the very issues that will be discussed in these programs. Our goal is to provide teenagers with an opportunity to consider their individual futures in relation to the collective future of the Jewish people and to make responsible Jewish decisions.

The teenagers in your group will probably expect their future to be "neatly packaged." Most adolescents believe that love, marriage, a career, success, etc. will evolve automatically at the expected time. They are likely to see the decisions they will make in terms of absolutes: "I _would never_ do X" or "I _absolutely will_ do Y." It is important to help them understand that the future is not predetermined and that it is open to limitless possibilities and unexpected challenges.

Knowing where they stand and what they believe will help adolescents to meet the challenges they will encounter as they grow into adulthood. They need to know that we all feel differently about Judaism at various points in our lives: sometimes we feel closer, sometimes more disconnected. This understanding will help teenagers to explore their current beliefs fully and consider what they will mean for the years ahead.

The facilitator sets the tone of the program. Advance preparation and the desire to connect openly and honestly with participants will enable him/her to be flexible in responding to the needs of the group. Such openness invites the group to share more openly. Flexibility is particularly important because no two groups will respond in the same way to the program. It is appropriate for the facilitator to model an ongoing grappling with the issues that are being discussed. ("When I was in college, I thought...;" "I never thought it was easy to talk about..." etc.) As always, the facilitator should use personal material _sparingly_ and _thoughtfully_ to model behavior or to make a particular point. If the facilitator is open and honest, participants will find it easier to confront the issues more comfortably. Keep the focus of discussion on "how" and "why" rather than on "should not" and "cannot."

The teenagers in your group will inevitably make statements that will catch you off guard or distress you. When that happens, take care not to respond with hostility or severe judgments. Responses like, "That's a horrible thing to say!" or "And you came from a family that has such strong Jewish values!" say "You don't belong." _Facilitators have an obligation to make statements about Jewish values, but they must be presented in a way that teenagers will hear_. Responses like, "Let me explain why Jews feel so strongly about this" or "I sometimes worry that we don't take this issue seriously enough" or "Let me give you an example of what I'm talking about and why I think it's important" will promote discussion and keep the door open. Remember, few teenagers will admit publicly that they agree with you or that they fully embrace the values you're discussing. It's not in the code of accepted adolescent behavior!

Finally, let the group know that you are not there to tell them what to do. It is a program _about them_ and about how they feel about their own Jewishness. These programs are designed to help participants to explore some of the challenging questions that arise as a result of living as Reform Jews in the twentieth century. It is our hope that every Jewish young adult will choose a partner who is Jewish, but none of us can predict the future. By encouraging adolescents to grapple with who they are as Jews, we play an important role in preparing them for the future. They will be able to discuss with _any_ partner, Jewish or not, their perspectives on living a Jewish life and raising Jewish children.

Choosing a Program:
Experience suggests that these programs are best used in combination. It will be difficult for your group to discuss interdating or intermarriage in a vacuum if they have not had an opportunity to begin to clarify their own Jewish values. Before planning your program, read through the entire packet so that you have a sense of the full range of options available to you. You will notice that some of the programs can be categorized in more than one section (i.e., a values clarification exercise may relate to intermarriage, text study informs our Jewish values, etc.) Once you have a sense of what is available to you, consider the special talents of the facilitator and the needs of your particular group to guide your selection.

Appendix 1 (Programming Planning Worksheet) and **Appendix 2** (Program Evaluation Worksheet) can be useful in helping you plan your program. **Appendix 3** contains a program evaluation form.
Appendix 4 (What is Outreach?) provides a brief explanation of the Outreach program. **Appendix 5** provides suggestions for background reading and useful resources. **Appendix 6** lists the names of the Regional Outreach Coordinators. Your regional Outreach Coordinator can serve as an important resource in helping you to plan your program.

SECTION TWO

PART ONE

WARM-UP EXERCISES

PROGRAM 1A

Title: Prized Possessions

Objectives: 1. To promote group interaction

                2. To enable participants to begin to consider the meaning of their Jewishness

Time Required: Depending upon group size, between one-half hour and one hour

Materials Needed: None

Instructions for the Facilitator:

Ask participants to find a partner, preferably someone they don't know. When the group has divided into pairs, ask participants to think about something they own (or have owned in the past) which is special and has meaning only to them. Examples may include a blanket, a stuffed animal, a pressed flower, etc. Ask participants to tell their partners about the prized possession they have chosen, how they got it, what it means to them, what makes it special, and if they had ever really thought about or been asked why this object was so important to them. Provide about five minutes for each partner to speak, once partners have been selected and the group settles down.

You may choose to extend the exercise by reconvening the large group and asking participants to introduce their partner to the group by name and with several sentences about that person's prized possession. Example: "This is Sarah Green. Her prized possession is an old teddy bear with one eye missing that was given to her by her best friend in first grade. She loves it more than anything else she has." Introductions should be kept short. Important: if you plan to do this part of the exercise, be sure to tell participants at the beginning so that they will choose to describe possessions and circumstances that they will be comfortable sharing with the whole group.

Explain to the group that this exercise is a model for how you will be exploring Jewish identity in future programs. Our Jewishness was given to some of us at birth and to others by choice: either way, it is special to each of us in different ways. Most of us have probably never been asked to define how we feel about our Judaism -- what makes us feel safe, secure, and comforted, as well as why, at times, we may feel confused or ambivalent about our Jewish lives and the Jewish community.

PROGRAM 1B

Title: The Name Game

Objectives:
1. To promote group interaction
2. To enable participants to think about themselves in relation to their family
3. To provide participants with an opportunity to consider the connection between names and identity

Time Required: One-half hour minimum

Materials Needed: None

Instructions for the Facilitator:

1. You may want to make some preliminary remarks about the role names have played in Jewish life (name changes through immigration, loss of life and family names through the Holocaust, names that are easily identifiable as Jewish, reactions of Jews to "non-Jewish sounding" names within our community, why people choose to change names, vogue of certain names in generations, familiar names, etc.)

2. Instruct participants to divide into small groups. (Groups of four work well.) Ask one person in each group to serve as a recorder.

3. Participants should be instructed to talk with one another about their name. Discussion may include the meaning of the name in the family (pet names and nicknames), for whom participants may have been named and why, whether they think their name fits them, other people's reactions to their name (trouble with spelling, "You *are* just like Grandpa!", etc.)

4. You may end the exercise at this point or, depending on time and group size, continue with one of the following:

    a. When the larger group reconvenes, ask the recorder for each small group to summarize the issues they discussed about names and what they tell us about people, OR

b. Ask each participant to introduce the person next to him/her by name, adding one sentence based on remarks the person has made about his/her name. (Example: "This is Staci Goldstein, named after her grandmother Sophie, who was a wonderful and witty person," or "This is Marvin Abromovitz, whose family name used to be Liss until his grandfather changed it to Abromovitz because he thought it sounded more American!")

5. Summarize the significance of names in Jewish tradition. Give examples of how certain biblical names were changed to connote a change in destiny, eg. Abram to Abraham, Sarai to Sarah, Jacob to Israel.

Discuss the rabbinic saying that individuals are given three names: the name they are born with; the names others give them; and the names people give themselves.

The facilitator should be prepared to close the exercise with remarks about the roles names play for us. Others see us according to the role we play in their lives, ie. mother, father, sibling, friend, etc. The name _we_ choose reflects how we see ourselves in relationship to others.

When facilitating this exercise be sure that you are prepared with some thoughts about your own name to use as examples.

PROGRAM 1C

Title: Quotes Program

Objectives: 1.   To promote group cohesion

               2.   To engage participants in discussion of Jewish issues

Time Required: One hour

Materials Needed: Copies of the quotations

Instructions for the Facilitator:

This is a very easy program to run. It is also one of the best for helping the participants get to know one another and begin to express some of their own thoughts and feelings.

Divide participants into groups of five or six people.

Write each quote listed below on a separate piece of paper. Hand out one quote at a time, letting one person per group read it out loud to the group for reaction and discussion. Give participants 5-10 minutes for discussion of each quote before moving on to the next one.

The following quotes, which have each been assigned a number for easier use, range in content from a broader to a more personal tone. The facilitator should select a maximum of five quotes. You may certainly substitute favorite quotes of your own.

**The Sidney and Betty Jacobs' quotes were taken from their book, <u>122 Clues for Jews Whose Children Intermarry</u>. The remaining quotes were taken from <u>The Jewish Experiential Book</u>. Bernard Reisman. Ktav, NY, 1979.

QUOTES

#1

"If the statistics are right, the Jews constitute but one percent of the human race. It suggests a nebulous dim puff of star dust lost in the blaze of the Milky Way. Properly the Jew ought hardly to be heard of. He has made a marvelous fight in this world, in all the ages; and he has done it with his hands tied behind him." (Mark Twain)

#2

"Nothing pleases most Jews more than to be told they don't look Jewish or behave Jewishly, that they can not be distinguished in their appearance, dress, speech, attitudes or behavior from non-Jews." (Prof. Charles Liebman, Bar-Ilan University)

#3

"The center of Judaism is in the home. In contrast to other religions, it is at home where the essential celebrations and acts of observance take place - rather than in the synagogue or temple.... The synagogue is an auxiliary.... A Jewish home is where Judaism is at home, where Jewish learning, commitment, sensitivity to values are cultivated and cherished." (Abraham Joshua Heschel)

#4

(Speaking of an interfaith family): "If children should know about the heritage of both parents, shouldn't they celebrate the holidays of both, holidays such as Christmas and Hanukkah?" (Sidney and Betty Jacobs)

#5

"How about a couple who say that their religious differences make absolutely no difference to them, since neither one cares about religion?" (Sidney and Betty Jacobs)

#6

"I could never imagine Jews other than surrounded by Jews. In joy as in sorrow, a Jew is never alone.

"Just as man needs other men to be human, so does a Jew need other Jews to be Jewish. He chooses to define himself not in relation to the hate he elicits from strangers, but rather to the faith he inspires in his people.

"A Jew alone is a Jew in danger, a Jew inviting danger! His security lies within the community which helps him survive and attain fulfillment." (Elie Wiesel)

#7

"Aren't we all being too understanding? If the Jewish community were to stand firmly opposed to intermarriage, wouldn't it be less of a problem? It seems that all the books, workshops and "outreach" having to deal with intermarriage are almost rewarding those Jews who have turned their back on their people." (Sidney and Betty Jacobs)

#8

"The history of the Jews has been described as the Romance of a People, and the only meaningful relationship a Jew, by birth or conversion, can have with Judaism is to fall in love with it! So much of our time and energy is spent in Jewish organizational activity and so little in Jewish living that we forget to "romance" our Judaism. If we paid more attention to what the Jewish essence is, we would have far less confusion about the value of perpetuating it." (Sidney and Betty Jacobs)

SECTION TWO

PART TWO

PROGRAMS ON INTERDATING AND INTERMARRIAGE

PROGRAM 2A

Title: Intermarriage: A Modern Jewish Fairytale

Objective: To enable participants to begin to identify attitudes about intermarriage in a non-threatening, entertaining format.

Time Required: One-half hour

Materials Needed: A copy of the exercise for each participant, pencils or pens, a large pad with markers or a blackboard with chalk.

Instructions for the Facilitator:

Distribute the exercise and ask participants to read it first without writing, then to begin to fill in the blanks. Invite them to be creative and funny. Remind them to write legibly, since someone else will be reading their answers. Allow about ten minutes.

When participants have finished, collect the exercises and ask for several volunteers to read selected fairytales to the group. Explain that you will not be reading them all. It is recommended that the facilitator quickly skim each sheet before handing it to the volunteers in order to screen out any that may be offensive or hurtful to participants who may come from an intermarried home.

Ask for another volunteer to be the recorder. While the volunteers are reading the fairytales, the recorder lists on the board or large pad examples of the language used. (e.g., the Goldstein family faced a: <u>dilemma</u>, <u>crisis</u>, <u>tragedy</u>, <u>opportunity</u>, etc. The purpose is to look at the language used by participants, so it will be important to write as many examples on the board as possible. It is sometimes helpful to have two recorders.

When the volunteers have finished reading the fairytales selected, ask the group what they notice about their answers. What do the words they chose say about their attitudes? Where do their attitudes come from? Is what they have said accurate? What kinds of judgments are reflected in their answers? If their parents were filling in the blanks, how would their answers be different? What is the historical basis of Jewish attitudes toward intermarriage? As always, the facilitator should be careful to be sensitive to participants who may come from intermarried or conversionary families.

Finally, the facilitator should summarize the exercise by noting that even when we are purposely trying to have fun and be silly, our attitudes and assumptions emerge. Future programming on the topics of Jewish identity, Jewish values, and interdating and intermarriage will provide opportunities to consider the issues in more depth.

INTERMARRIAGE

A MODERN JEWISH FAIRYTALE

Once upon a time, not a very long time ago, the Goldstein family faced a _____. Their daughter Staci, who was beautiful, smart, wonderful, and _____, announced that she had decided to marry a _____ young man named _____. Mrs. Goldstein was _____, and she told Staci that intermarriage almost always_____.

She feared that her own mother, Bubie Goldstein, would _____ _____. (Bubie's actual reaction to the news was _____ _____.) Mr. Goldstein said to Staci, "Why can't you be like your cousin Sarah who is marrying _____?" (Staci didn't tell him that Sarah's fiancé _____ _____!)

Staci's friends advised her to _____ because they _____. The Goldsteins were_____ to talk with their rabbi, who advised them to_____because_____Staci's fiancé thought all of this was a bit _____.

The moral of the story is _____ _____.

And they all lived_____ever after.

33

PROGRAM 2B

Title: "Mary and Herb"

Objective: To broaden participants' understanding of the dilemmas that may be encountered in an intermarriage

Time Required: Thirty to forty minutes

Materials Needed: Scenario, pencils and paper

Instructions for the Facilitator:

This exercise can be done individually, in pairs or in small groups. It is important to insure that all categories are included. If the exercise is done individually, in pairs or in small groups, the participants then return to the larger group to report. The facilitator should not answer any questions regarding specifics of the scenario and should state that the exercise is deliberately ambiguous. Participants may be frustrated if unable to come up with a "solution" and will sometimes state that this is an extreme case. It may be helpful to respond that it is dramatic, but that the feelings and the dilemma are common.

* * *

Mary and Herb Kushner have just had their first child, a boy. They have never discussed birth rituals previously, feeling that they would make the necessary decisions when the time came. Now that their son is born, they are aware of very strong feelings on the part of both sets of parents. Herb's parents are concentration camp survivors who lost their entire families in the Holocaust. They are very excited about the <u>brit milah</u> (ritual circumcision) that they are sure will be held for their new grandson. Mary's father, Edward O'Brian, is dying of cancer. He has been a good Catholic all his life, and he has expressed a strong desire to have his grandson baptized.

Please discuss the situation with your group, considering the following:

1. What are the <u>feelings</u> of each person above? (When in doubt, imagine!)

2. What should Mary and Herb do? List three possible solutions or approaches.

3. List three <u>funny</u> solutions. (Be outrageous!)

4. Select the best solution from the above and be prepared to discuss your choice and reasoning with the group.

Program 2C

Title: Insights Into Intermarriage

Objectives: 1.   To enable participants to explore issues relating to intermarriage

2.   To sensitize participants to the needs of non-Jewish spouses and to explore ways to include them in synagogue life

Time Required: Forty-five minutes to one hour

Materials Needed: A copy of the poem for each participant

Instructions for the Facilitator:

The following poem was written by a non-Jewish woman who is married to a Jew and is raising her children as Jews in a Reform Temple. Read the poem out loud. Ask participants for initial reactions. Encourage participants to ask questions. Possible discussion questions are included.

The following poem was written by a non-Jewish woman who is married to a Jew and is raising her children as Jews in a Reform temple.

Look. See. You're not so different from me.
You fear me.
You ask yourself how to prevent me from striking and
 penetrating your community.
What will happen to my Judaism, to my children?
Careful!
I can't speak freely anymore within my sweet temple
Foreigners trespass here.

Look. See. You're not so different from me.
I am the foreigner who lives with you.
I gave you children.
I usurped the role of a Jewish mother.
I answer my children's questions about the
 Almighty One.
Yet you deny me the equality of my presence.
You discount my gifts and friendship.
You convey the message that a tragedy befell you which
 shakes the solidity
I try to provide our children.
You deny that another foreign heritage has nurtured you
 and aids in your perpetuation.

Look. See. You're not so different from me.
We share the same God,
the same blood,
the same vulnerabilities,
the same sensitivities
the same capacity for pain,
the same children.

Look. See. You're not so different from me.
I fear you as you fear me.
You fear being looked upon as unaccepting,
 unwelcoming, unloving.
Where do you draw the line?
You see the foreigner has grown to be aware of the same
 fears, the same questions, the same doubts when
 speaking up to ameliorate our differences.

Look. See. You're not so different from me.
But why can't we live in easy harmony?
Why the need to quarrel over semantics?
Why the need to possess?
Why can't we share, support, appreciate,
And love each other for the diverse richness we each
 contribute?

Look. See. You're not so different from me.
God loves you and God loves me.
God hears you and God hears me.
God loves the double background with which we nurture
    our children.
"He" is the focus nothing more.
"He" hears our shared prayers in all their color and
    disguises.

Look. See. You're not so different from me.
No one asks you to lose so don't ask me.
There must be a place for me to grow in comfort and
    dignity.

                                                            Linda Rosolio Klein

Excerpted from: <u>Outreach and the Changing Reform Jewish Community:
Creating an Agenda for Our Future</u> (UAHC,1989). Reprinted with
permission.

Discussion Questions:

1. How does the writer of this poem feel about the Jewish community? How does she think the Jewish community feels about her? What does the author think we fear about her presence in the Jewish community? What is making her feel uncomfortable (unwelcome) in the Jewish community? What are the greatest fears of the Jewish community?

2. What about the author's presence and involvement in the Jewish community makes us uncomfortable? What messages do you think we are sending out to non-Jewish spouses? What should be our message to non-Jewish spouses?

3. Can we accept the fact that some people can become very much a part of the life of our community but choose not to convert?

4. Why do people decide not to become Jewish while still affiliating on some level with the Jewish community?

5. There are non-Jews who are married to Jews who choose to raise their children as Jews even though they themselves do not convert. Is an unconverted mother capable of raising Jewish children? Will her children have as "authentic" a Jewish experience as those children who are being raised by parents who are both Jewish? How does a Jewish child respond to a parent who has chosen not to convert, and who may even be practicing a different religion?

6. What is the role of the Jewish mother today? How is the contemporary Jewish mother different from her own mother or grandmother? What will characterize the Jewish mother of the future?

    How do couples make decisions about the religious upbringing of their children?

7. How can we become more sensitive to intermarried couples, and in particular to the non-Jewish spouse, who affiliate with Jewish community?

8. What does the author have in common with the Jewish community?

9. What might be done to encourage the writer to convert? Is this an appropriate goal?

PROGRAM 2D

Title: Interdating: Responding To The Issues

Objectives: 1.   To explore issues relating to intermarriage and interdating from the perspective of the parent, the young person and the non-Jewish partner

2. To encourage participants to identify some of the challenges and difficulties of interfaith relationships and to think through how they might deal with them

Time Required: One hour

Materials Needed: A copy of the scenarios for each participant

Instructions for the Facilitator:

Three scenarios are provided to serve as discussion starters. They may be discussed in small groups or role played. If the scenarios are role played, volunteers may be asked to step in mid-stream to act out the part in a different way.

An interesting twist to this program might be to have parents play the role of the teens and the teens play the role of the parents. It is important to note that while generalizations may sometimes be made, different individuals will respond very differently to the same role play. Not every Jewish teenager, friend, mother, father, Christian friend etc. will take the same position.

1. For each scenario, assign parts. Provide the role players with a copy of their particular scenario. Allow 5 minutes for participants to prepare the role play. If time allows, parts may be assigned prior to the actual program so the participants can have more time to prepare.

2. The role play, which may be 5-10 minutes in length, is presented to the entire group. If the group is on the large side, divide into smaller discussion groups of 8-10, assigning a facilitator to each group. It is most effective to prepare facilitators in advance by meeting with them to discuss some of the issues that might be raised through discussion and to brainstorm ways to respond. Reconvene the larger group and have a representative of each group report on the issues raised in their discussion.

3. Summarize and wrap up discussion.

Discussion:

1. What was it like to play out these situations?

2. Why is it important to discuss the issues raised by these role plays?

3. Is it such a big deal to interdate? Isn't adolescence the time of life to experiment?

4. The truth of the matter is that some of you are interdating and may even intermarry. How does the Jewish community respond to intermarried couples? Why? How should the Jewish community respond to intermarried couples? Why?

5. In what way is each and every one of us responsible for the future of Judaism and the Jewish people?

The Scenarios

A. Shelley Steinhart is a sixteen year old junior in high school who lives in an area where there are very few Jews. In her school there are only three Jewish boys her age or older. One is involved in a relationship with another girl, and neither of the other two Jewish boys are attractive to her. Shelley comes from a very Jewishly committed family, and her parents have always emphasized the importance of dating Jews. You are her best friend, and she has come to you to talk. She feels her life is passing her by. She sees her only options as either staying home from social events, which she has done in the past, or dating someone who is not of interest just because he's Jewish. What will you advise Shelley to do?

Discussion Questions:

1. Shelley sees her options as "staying home" or "dating someone who is not of interest just because he's Jewish." What other alternatives might be open to her?

2. How should Shelley approach her parents to discuss her dilemma? What should she say to them? What do you think their reaction might be?

3. What implications does Shelley's dilemma have for her plans to attend college?

ALTERNATIVE PROGRAM IDEAS:

Read the scenario aloud and ask students to volunteer to role play. Ask two students to volunteer to role play the conversation between Shelley and her friend, and/or ask three students to role play a problem-solving discussion between Shelley and her parents. Discuss.

B. Rob Halpern is in his freshman year at a college far from his home town. He has found it very hard to make friends, but he has fallen in love with Beth, who comes from an evangelical Christian background. Beth is deeply religious while Rob, since he left home, isn't quite sure how he feels about Judaism. He hasn't attended any Jewish activities on campus. Beth has not mentioned Rob's Judaism, but she has asked him to attend church services with her on several occasions, which he has declined. Although they have not discussed the possibility of marriage, both view their relationship as a long-term one. Neither has told his/her parents about the other.

Discussion Questions:

1. What does "evangelical" mean? What are the implications for Rob and Beth's relationship?

2. What stumbling blocks will Rob and Beth face if their relationship does become long-term?

3. Given that they are from such different backgrounds, what are some of the reasons Rob and Beth might have been attracted to one another?

4. Why haven't Rob and Beth really discussed religion, especially since it is obviously such an important issue?

5. How might Rob and Beth begin to explore what their religious differences might mean for their future?

6. Should they talk with their parents? Why/Why not?

ALTERNATIVE PROGRAM IDEAS:

Read the scenario aloud and ask students to volunteer to role play. Ask two students to volunteer to role play a conversation between Rob and Beth in which Rob explains why he has not agreed to go to church with her. Two students might also role play Rob and his best friend from home, who is also Jewish, discussing Beth and her religious background. Volunteers might also role play a conversation between Beth and her parents, and then again between Rob and his parents. How are the conversations similar? Different?

C. You have been asked to plan a workshop for the confirmation class at your temple on interdating and intermarriage. It will be a one-evening program, and you may use your rabbi and the regional Outreach Coordinator as resources. Since a program like this has never been done at your temple and it may be somewhat controversial, you want it to be great! Talk with your planning committee and begin to organize the event.

Discussion Questions:

1. What should the Reform community say to its teenagers about interdating and intermarriage? In one sentence, what should the central message of your workshop be?

2. What questions will you want to ask your rabbi? The Outreach Coordinator?

3. Why is the Jewish community so concerned about intermarriage? What historical background will be important for participants to know?

4. Should parents be included in the workshop? Why/Why not?

5. What should parents be told about how to talk to teenagers about the subject?

6. What do you think the participants will want the Jewish community to understand about the perspectives of its teenagers on the subject?

7. From the point of view of the confirmation class, what ingredients will be needed in order for this to be a successful program?

ALTERNATIVE PROGRAM IDEAS:

Ask participants to take turns, for one minute each, role playing the presenter at the workshop. They are to talk to the group about the perspective of the Jewish community on interdating and intermarriage. Keep a list on the blackboard of the points made. (This is likely to cause preliminary stage fright and will probably include some humor.) After everyone has had a turn, discuss the points made. Are they accurate? Do they understand the perspective of the Reform community and the Outreach program? Identify positive components and highlight any missing information or inaccuracies. Ask the group to note any specific statements that made their ability to hear the message easier.

PROGRAM 2E

Title: <u>Intermarriage: When Love Meets Tradition</u>

Objective: To discuss the implications of interdating, intermarriage and Jewish identity.

Time Required: One and one-half hours

Materials Needed: <u>Intermarriage: When Love Meets Tradition</u> (video) and discussion guide

Instructions for the Facilitator:

This program begins with a <u>brief</u> explanation of the Outreach program and an introduction to the film: <u>Intermarriage: When Loves Meets Tradition</u>. (This 33 minute film is available in both 16 mm and 1/2" VHS at special low rates to UAHC congregations. Order films directly from Direct Cinema, Ltd., P.O. Box 69799, Los Angeles, CA 90069, or call (213) 653-8000. For further information, call your UAHC Regional office.)

After the film is shown, divide the group into smaller sections (about 10/group) and use the following discussion guide. Discussion can be led by temple youth group (TYG) seniors. (An excellent in-depth study guide is available for $2.00 from the National Outreach Office in New York.)

Following the discussion, have the entire group come together for a wrap-up to respond to remaining questions.

The facilitator should introduce the program and film, as well as lead the wrap-up. It is advisable for the facilitator to meet in advance with the people leading the small section discussion groups to consider the best way to facilitate the discussion. Suggestions for who might serve as the facilitator include: Regional Outreach Coordinator, rabbi, mental health professional, or trained lay leader who has good group skills and a solid Jewish background.

<u>Note</u>: There will probably be teens in your group whose parents are intermarried. It is especially important to be careful about making negative generalizations about intermarriage. Use phrases like "<u>Some</u> intermarried couples...," "Intermarriage <u>sometimes</u> means," "Intermarried people <u>may</u> feel," etc. Do not ask directly who has intermarried parents, but gently encourage everyone to talk by asking question #2. Remember: teens from intermarried homes may feel anxious about this program. It is crucial that participants receive one message from this program: YOU BELONG HERE.

44

Discussion Questions:

1. What did you think of this film? (Ask for initial reactions. OK to discuss whether teens feel it is anti-intermarriage propaganda. If some do feel that way, ask why they think such a film was made. What is the message of the film intended to be? Where did that message come from?)

2. Ask the group who in their family or social circle has intermarried. How long ago? What was the result in terms of that person's relationship with family, friends, Jewish community? Do they think there is a difference in attitude now as opposed to 10, 20, 30 years ago?

3. What did you think about the parents on the film? (See "Common Comments and Responses," which follows) What do parents have a right to say to their children about interdating and intermarriage? What shouldn't they say?

4. How are the parents on the film similar to or different from yours? What messages have your parents given you about interdating and intermarriage? (Some participants will say their parents haven't said anything, but they know where their parents stand. How do they know? What have been the "covert" messages about the topic?)

5. What are the major obstacles that interfaith couples have to deal with? Use the couples on film as an example. Are these obstacles similar to what Jewish couples must deal with? Why? Why not?

6. Which couple on the film, in your opinion, has the greatest chance for "success?" (See "Common Comments and Responses") Which couple seems the most troubled? (Be sure to note that the problems are relationship issues that the couples themselves have raised. They are NOT problems superimposed by parents' negativity. Example: Eve-Lynn and Michael.)

7. List on the board qualities that the group looks for in someone to date (Fun to be with, popular, same interests, etc.) Make a separate list of qualities they will look for in someone to marry. Is there any overlap? Does "Jewish" appear? Why or why not?

8. What issues came up that were new to you? Why is this issue so important to the Jewish community? What else can we do in addition to tonight's discussion to make sure that these issues are talked about in our families and in our classrooms?

COMMON COMMENTS AND RESPONSES:

I. <u>Jewish Teenagers</u>

    A. "I think it's alright to interdate, but I won't intermarry."

    <u>Response</u>: This is a common misconception of teenagers. It is important to explore with them the connection between interdating and intermarriage, a connection they do not always make. The film successfully documents many of the difficulties interfaith couples face. Emphasize the points articulated by each of the couples in the film about the conflict of wanting to be with someone they love and wanting to have a Jewish home and to pass the Jewish heritage to the next generation.

    B. "Eve-Lynn's mother gives her daughter a guilt trip."

    <u>Response</u>: Explore with the group parents' dilemma of loving their child but not always agreeing with their child's choices. We don't always like to hear that our parents disagree with us, but Eve-Lynn's mother asks difficult questions which help Eve-Lynn clarify what she needs. What are some of the ways parents pass on specific values? Is this done verbally or through actions?

    C. "Annette and Ira are not cool, but Laurel and Mark really have it together."

    <u>Response</u>: Teenagers often compare the couples in the film. Do not allow the group to dwell on the couples themselves. Instead, focus on the issues brought out by the film.

PROGRAM 2F

Title: **This Great Difference**

Objective: To discuss the implications of interdating, intermarriage and Jewish identity

Time Required: One and one-half hours

Materials Needed: **This Great Difference** (video) and discussion guide

Instructions for the Facilitator:

This program begins with a brief explanation of the Outreach program and an introduction to the trigger film, **This Great Difference**. (This 13-minute film is available in both 16 mm and 1/2" VHS video at special low rates to UAHC congregations. Order films directly from Direct Cinema Ltd., P.O. Box 69799, Los Angeles, CA 90069, or call (213) 653-8000. For further information, call your UAHC Regional office).

After the film is shown, divide the group into smaller sections (about 10/group) and use the attached discussion guide for discussion, which can be led by temple youth group (TYG) seniors.

Following the discussion, have the entire group come together for a wrap-up to respond to remaining questions.

The facilitator should introduce the program and film, as well as lead the wrap-up. It is advisable for the facilitator to meet in advance with the people leading the small group discussion to plan the best way to facilitate the discussion. Suggestions for who might serve as the facilitator include: Regional Outreach Coordinator, rabbi, mental health professional, or trained lay leader who has good group skills and a solid Jewish background.

A DISCUSSION GUIDE FOR "THIS GREAT DIFFERENCE"
(Interdating and Intermarriage; sub-theme of Jewish Continuity)

1. Eve-Lynn's mother comes down pretty heavily on the side of Jewish continuity. She says: "We bring into the world something the world needs and that's worthwhile. And we're such a pitiful minority, that if Jews don't see that and make that selection, there will not be any more Jews."

    Do you agree or disagree?
    Did you ever discuss this with your parents?
    What do your parents say?
    Do you think they would mind if you went on a date with a non-Jew?

2. Eve-Lynn says: "I'm trying with all my heart to hold onto my Jewishness and the man I love. I don't want to give up either one." Another name for this film might be "When Love Meets Tradition."

    What did Eve-Lynn feel toward the man she loves? What pulls does she feel toward her Judaism? (Be specific: chupah, breaking glass, familiarity with service, brit milah for son, etc.)

3. Eve-Lynn says that going to church with Michael was "alien." "There was so much talk of Jesus--Jeez." Michael finds the Jewish ceremonies that are so important to Eve-Lynn "noise."

    Have you ever been to church? How did it feel?
    Have you ever brought a non-Jewish girlfriend or boyfriend to services or to another Jewish event? How do you think they felt? How did you feel? Is there a difference between inter-religious friendship and interdating?
    Why? or why not?

4. Eve-Lynn says that just as she could never convert, Michael will never convert. "That's not who he is."

    Can one person ask another to convert?
    How would the situation change for Michael and Eve-Lynn if one of them wanted to convert?

***   Note: Do not force participants to respond to any question. There may be participants who are children of intermarriage or who have very positive feelings about relatives who are intermarried. First, support the worth of each participant. Suggest that there may be an extra measure of effort and compromise required to make an intermarriage work.

Excerpted from: Reform Jewish Outreach: The Idea Book (UAHC, 1988). Reprinted with permission.

PROGRAM 2G

Title: Choosing a Partner: Asking the Right Questions

Objectives: 1. To explore issues relating to interdating and intermarriage

              2. To encourage participants to explore their own feelings about the person they hope to marry, their religious beliefs and the religious identity they plan to give to their children

              3. To strengthen communication skills

Time Required: One hour

Materials Needed: None

Instructions for the Facilitator:

This program is designed to encourage participants to explore openly and honestly their feelings about some difficult issues. It is important that the facilitator and setting chosen foster a safe and comfortable environment.

The following discussion questions can be used to stimulate discussion. Encourage participants to be as specific as possible when responding.

The (*) indicates that the question applies only to college-age participants. Non-Jewish partners may be invited to participate.

Discussion Questions:

1. How does dating a non-Jew differ from dating a Jew? Do these differences bother you?

2. Does interdating bring about a conflict of love vs. loyalty?

3. Are you less than faithful to your religion if you interdate? Why/why not?

4. What is your family's attitude toward interdating?

5. What have your parents said directly about interdating and intermarriage? What indirect messages have they sent?

*6. What kind of connection do you have with the Jewish community?

   For the non-Jew: What kind of connection do you have with your religious community?

*7. What in your Judaism is important to you?

   For the non-Jew: What in your religion is important to you?

*8. How many of you would consider marriage at this point if you found the right person? What kind of relationship do you envision having with your spouse?

9. Do you think it is important to marry someone who is Jewish (or who shares the same religious beliefs and ethnocultural background)? Why/why not?

10. Do you plan to have children? How do you plan to raise your children?

11. Do you feel that it is important to pass on your Jewish heritage? Is it possible in an interfaith relationship?

*12. Do you think your partner would feel comfortable raising the children as Jews?

*13. Have you spoken with your partner about religion, how you would want to raise your children, the home you would like to create, etc.? If not, why not?

14. What assumptions regarding religion do you tend to make about the person you will someday marry?

15. How might differences in parents' religions affect the way the children identify religiously?

16. How might you resolve religious differences if you intermarried?

SECTION TWO

PART THREE

REFORM JEWISH IDENTITY AND VALUES CLARIFICATION

PROGRAM 3A

Title: Jewish Values: A Personal Inventory

Objective: To enable participants to consider the personal importance of Judaism for them. (This exercise works well as a prelude to a program on interdating or intermarriage).

Time Required: One and one-half hours

Materials Needed: A copy of the exercise for each participant; a copy of the discussion questions for each small group leader; pens or pencils

Instructions for the Facilitator:

The facilitator begins by remarking to the group that it is sometimes difficult for us to know exactly what aspects of Judaism are most important to us. Our ideas about religion change as we grow: the Jewishness of the teenagers in the group is probably quite different from their sense of themselves as Jews in early childhood. It is important for the facilitator to "normalize" the range of response to various aspects of Jewish belief and practice at different times in our lives. Reform Judaism began with the recognition that religion must be meaningful to the individual and relevant to the times in which we live. We have always embraced the need to personalize Judaism. This exercise provides an opportunity to begin to clarify our individual Jewish values.

The "Jewish Values: A Personal Inventory" sheets should be distributed to the group. Instruct participants to answer honestly and avoid the temptation to provide answers that their teachers/rabbi/advisor/peers may want to hear. Provide about 10 minutes for participants to finish.

Jewish Values: A Personal Inventory

Directions: Please fill tn the blanks with "T" (True) or "F" (False):

_____In social situations, I usually identify myself as a Jew.

_____There are situations in which religion isn't an issue and should not be raised as one.

_____I feel a strong commitment to the State of Israel and its welfare.

_____Organized religion is important to my family.

_____My family celebrates Shabbat in some fashion each week.

_____I probably will be religiously observant when I am an adult.

_____Some people are too religious.

_____Only my Jewish friends really understand me.

_____I only date other Jews.

_____In most cases, the problems of intermarried couples are minimal.

_____Celebrating Jewish holidays with my family is important to me.

_____It is very difficult for non-Jews to understand the full meaning of the Holocaust.

_____I feel comfortable celebrating Christmas.

_____I would like to be married in a Jewish ceremony with a rabbi officiating.

Discussion Guide

Note to the facilitator: If your group is large, break the group down into smaller groups of 6-8 participants. Each group should appoint a discussion leader, who is given a copy of the following discussion guide and is responsible for keeping the group discussion on track. The discussion leader will report back to the larger group when it reconvenes.

1. What initial response did you have to this exercise? Did you find it difficult? Easy?

2. Did any of the questions elicit a strong reaction, positive or negative, when you read it? Which one(s)? Why?

3. Did the exercise raise any questions you hadn't considered before?

4. Were you consistent in your responses?

5. For those of you who answered "F" to the question about Israel, what reaction do you have when you hear non-Jews criticize Israel? What do you think is the source of your response?

6. Have there been situations in which you preferred that people not know that you are Jewish? Explain.

7. For those of you who said you were not comfortable celebrating Christmas, what makes you feel uncomfortable?

8. For those of you who date people of other religious backgrounds, how do you see this fitting into your future? During college? Afterward?

9. Are there particular issues that have come up in discussion that have been difficult? Why?

10. How could the congregations/youth group/ religious school etc. better help teenagers to talk about these issues?

11. What should the message of the Reform Jewish Community be regarding interdating and intermarriage?

Note to the facilitator: When the large group reconvenes, the discussion leaders summarize what happened in their particular group. After all reports have been heard, the facilitator closes discussion by commenting on the range of issues that arose, agreement or differences of opinion among participants, and the need for continued dialogue on the issue of "personalizing Judaism."

PROGRAM 3B

Title: Choosing Judaism: What Do We Believe?

Objectives: 1.   To explore what the participants believe is central to their Judaism

2.   To draw parallels between participants' commitments and those made by Jews-by-Choice

3.   To introduce to the group what the UAHC has been doing in terms of Outreach (and how it relates to their lives)

Time Required: Two to two and one-half hours

Materials Needed: Fill-in the blank exercise
Paper for every participant
List of ten commitments for each group leader
Ten commitments on individual pieces of heavy paper for each group
Ten commitments written in very large letters on big sheet of paper
Pencils
Sample description of a Jew-by-Choice
Markers
Rabbi's Manual (CCAR, 1988)

Instructions for the Facilitator:

Part I (15 minutes)

Introduction of the program by facilitator (regional Outreach staff member, rabbi, educator, TYG advisor, etc.).

Divide into smaller groups, assigning a faculty leader to each group.

Hand out the fill-in-the-blank exercise and ask each participant to fill it out. There is to be no discussion or talking at this point. Assure participants that this is an anonymous fill-in-the-blank exercise. There are no right or wrong answers. Do not worry if you cannot fill in every blank. Allow three minutes for the completion of this exercise. Have group leaders collect the papers and put them aside. They will be used later in the program.

Part II (15 minutes)

The group leader presents to the group a "typical" Jew-by-Choice (see following description). Brainstorm with the group a list of the six most important questions a rabbi should ask a person who is seeking to convert to Judaism. What are they as Jews interested in learning and/or demanding from someone who is seeking to choose Judaism? Discuss their choice of questions. Have the group select six questions which they agree on.

A Typical Convert: Jane Harris is a 27 year-old nurse who works at a hospital on Long Island. She was raised a Catholic. While she still celebrates Christmas and Easter with her family in New York, she does not belong to a church. Her family is very close and she has a very good relationship with them. Jane has never been married and has been dating Michael Levy for the past two years. He is 31 years old, never married and is one of the administrators at the same hospital at which Jane works. He is Jewish and feels very strongly about his Judaism. He has not joined a synagogue, but he does attend services every so often at nearby synagogues. His family lives in Merrick and is very involved in their synagogue.

Jane and Michael are thinking of getting married. They went to a local rabbi, who suggested that Jane take an Introduction to Judaism class run by the UAHC Outreach program. Jane and Michael took the class together. They also attended services together on a fairly regular basis. Jane met with the rabbi during the course of the class. After completing the class, she decided to convert and has come to the rabbi to discuss the requirements for conversion. One of the requirements the rabbi explains is that there will be a ceremony, public or private, in which Jane will be asked to respond positively to six questions considered important in affirming her desire to become Jewish. What questions would our group ask Jane?

Part III (15 minutes)

Each group leader presents the six questions from the CCAR Rabbi's Manual (p.201) conversion service that are asked at the time of conversion. Discuss with the group the differences and similarities between the participants' questions and the questions listed in the Rabbi's Manual. Discuss the rabbis' selection of questions.

<u>Rabbi's Manual Questions</u>:

1. Do you choose to enter the eternal covenant between God and the people Israel and to become a Jew of your own free will?

2. Do you accept Judaism to the exclusion of all other religious faiths and practices?

3. Do you pledge your loyalty to Judaism and to the Jewish people under all circumstances?

4. Do you promise to establish a Jewish home, and to participate actively in the life of the synagogue and of the Jewish community?

5. Do you commit yourself to the pursuit of Torah and Jewish knowledge?

6. If you should be blessed with children, do you promise to raise them as Jews?

* * * *

NOTE: If additional time is available, a discussion about conversion might be interesting. The following are examples of discussion questions that might be used, though some may be a bit difficult for high school youth:

a. What does it mean to convert to another religion? For Christians? For Jews?

b. What are some of the losses, gains and pressures one experiences when choosing to convert?

c. What is involved in the conversion process (education, Jewish experiences and involvement, separating from former religion, "feeling" Jewish, etc.).

d. Assume you are the Jewish partner in an interfaith relationship, and your partner chooses to become Jewish.

1) What is your responsibility to your partner during (and after) the conversion process?

2) What are your concerns and, perhaps, fears?

3) Would you feel ambivalent or uncomfortable about it in any way?

e. What might be the reaction of your family toward this newly Jewish person?

What might be the reaction of this person's non-Jewish family?

f. How might you offer support during this process? How should you handle your family's and your partner's family's feelings?

g. How might you respond to the following question posed by someone considering conversion:

"One of the things I find attractive about Reform Judaism is that the religion permits flexibility and diversity in terms of belief and observance. What are the limits of this flexibility? What must a Jew believe and do in order to be Jewish?"

* * * *

Part IV (15 minutes)

Present the group with the list of Ten Commitments. Discuss them. Have the group arrange the ten commitments in their order of importance. (Each group's selections will be tallied at the end of the program.

Part V (35 minutes)

Return to the fill-in-the-blank exercise and look at the kinds of difficulties and positive feelings the participants have concerning Judaism. Draw parallels to the path of those who choose Judaism as adults. Draw on the earlier parts of this program for this discussion. Note that these questions ask us to struggle with some challenging issues regarding our Jewish identity. Everyone involved in an interfaith relationship or contemplating conversion must also grapple with these issues.

Reconvene the larger group. The facilitator will summarize the points and issues raised.

Tally the results of the Ten Commitments exercise and report to the group on their group priorities for Jewish living.

NOTE: The facilitator should be available throughout the program to answer questions about conversion, etc.

This is an anonymous fill-in -the-blank exercise. There are no right or wrong answers. Complete the following as best you can.

1. I am a Jew who _____.

2. The single most important ingredient in establishing a strong sense of Jewish identity is_____.

3. The most negative aspect of contemporary Jewish life is _____.

4. _____ should be a part of every American Jew's life.

5. Belief in God is _____ to the Jewish future.

6. You don't have to be _____ to be a good Jew.

7. The most important characteristic for a successful rabbi to have is _____.

8. The most fulfilling part of my own Jewish identity is_____ _____.

9. If I were honest, I would admit that the part of my Jewishness that I feel most uncomfortable about is _____.

10. The best reason to convert to Judaism is _____.

    The worst reason is _____.

YOM KIPPUR OBSERVANCE: Fasting & attending synagogue symbolic of commitment to observe the High Holidays and the Festivals.	**LIGHT SHABBAT CANDLES:** Symbolizes commitment to begin to observe Shabbat at home and in the synagogue.
MEZUZAH Symbolizes commitment to having a Jewish home.	**TZEDAKAH** Commitment to giving of self; time or money, according to ability.
DIETARY LAWS Accept some aspect that reflects understanding of their importance for Jewish life. The validity of the discipline. May begin with commitment to eat matzah on Passover.	**WORSHIP** Commitment to a regular worship experience; to be negotiated.
LOVE OF ISRAEL The Jewish people and the Land of Israel as the historical Jewish homeland and the Jewish State. Support the United Jewish Appeal or other organization(s) that act on behalf of Israel and Jews in America and around the world.	**RAISE CHILDREN AS JEWS** Commitment to "teach them faithfully to your children" (the V'ahavta prayer). To raise children in the Jewish tradition.
AFFILIATION Commitment to join a synagogue and become an active member of the synagogue community.	**EDUCATION** Must present an outline or plan for continuing a Jewish education.

PROGRAM 3C

Title: Making a Commitment to Judaism

Objectives:
1. To allow young people to feel "okay" about being who they are Jewishly.
2. To address the "all or nothing" syndrome which serves to deflate the Jewish self-esteem of a significant number of our teens.
3. To explore Reform Judaism and what makes it an authentic expression of Jewish living by discussing the commitment we make to Judaism through living Jewishly and performing certain Jewish acts.

Time Required: One to one and one-half hours

Materials Needed: Resource sheet for each participant, cut up into individual commitment cards

Instructions for the Facilitator:

The following resource sheet contains ten commitments to Judaism that some Jews-by-Choice have been asked by their rabbi to make.

Photocopy one copy for each participant. Before handing out, cut up into individual cards, one commitment per card. Give one packet of cards to each participant. Instruct each participant, working individually, to prioritize these commitments. Reconvene the group and have each participant explain the order they chose. Discuss.

Discuss which of these commitments currently plays an important role in the participants lives and which will probably play an important role in the future.

Explain that many people take an intellectual approach to Judaism, which is based on thought and belief rather than deed and action. The truth is that our actions can bring us closer to Judaism. Which of these commitments involve action? Which connect our senses: taste, touch, etc. to Judaism? Increased involvement in Judaism leads to a heightened spiritual experience.

Ask if anyone knows what kinesthetic learning is. Explain that it is a form of learning which encourages emotional and physical involvement. Many of these commitments are linked to kinesthetic learning.

Ask the participants if they have ever thought about or discussed their own personal involvement in Judaism. What is the basis for the Jewish choices they have made? What is involved in making choices?

Move the discussion to an exploration of some of the particular commitments. For example:

1. How do you define Shabbat? Can you think of anything you do on Friday night or Saturday that is special or different from what you do during the rest of the week? Perhaps a family meal, time with a friend, reading a book, taking a nap, playing ball - anything. From now on try to think of these actions not as what you do on Saturday, but what you want to do on <u>Shabbat</u>. In time you may add some traditional observances to your Shabbat. It is a start to begin seeing your own Shabbat as being special and Jewish, and to value the special things you do on this day.

2. What about dietary laws? Why are they included on this list of commitments? Does this mean that to be a good Jew one must keep kosher? Are there different levels of kashrut? What is the purpose of kashrut?

    How many of you eat matzah on Passover? How many of you fast on Yom Kippur? How many of you eat challah on Friday night? How many of you can think of a special meal your family always eats on certain holidays?

    How does the above relate to dietary laws?

3. Conclude by asking the participants to discuss these commitments with their family and friends and to begin to consider how they could live a more involved Jewish life.

YOM KIPPUR OBSERVANCE:

Fasting & attending synagogue - symbolic of commitment to observe the High Holidays and the Festivals.

MEZUZAH

Symbolizes commitment to having a Jewish home.

DIETARY LAWS

Accept some aspect that reflects understanding of their importance for Jewish life. The validity of the discipline. May begin with commitment to eat matzah on Passover.

LOVE OF ISRAEL

The Jewish people and the Land of Israel as the historical Jewish homeland and the Jewish State. Support the United Jewish Appeal or other organization(s) that act on behalf of Israel and Jews in America and around the world.

AFFILIATION

Commitment to join a synagogue and become an active member of the synagogue community.

LIGHT SHABBAT CANDLES:

Symbolizes commitment to begin to observe Shabbat at home and in the synagogue.

TZEDAKAH

Commitment to giving of self; time or money, according to ability.

WORSHIP

Commitment to a regular worship experience; to be negotiated.

RAISE CHILDREN AS JEWS

Commitment to "teach them faithfully to your children" (the V'ahavta prayer). To raise children in the Jewish tradition.

EDUCATION

Must present an outline or plan for continuing a Jewish education.

PROGRAM 3D

Title: Choosing Judaism: Dealing With Gain and Loss

Objective: To sensitize participants to some of the issues faced by new Jews as they choose Judaism.

Time Required: One to one and one-half hours

Materials Needed: One copy of the essay for each participant

Instructions for the facilitator:

> Explain that the essay which they are about to read out loud was written by a Jew-by-Choice:

Reflections

Giving up Christmas does not make me feel that my children will be deprived of the wonderful joys of that season. Lights and decorations abound at that time of year and my children will visit my parents every Christmas and unwrap presents from under the tree. They will not feel deprived because they will never know the feeling of having Christmas in their home.

Giving up Christmas is a loss to me. It's a loss that fills me with great sadness. I am the only one that will feel the emptiness and deprivation of not having Christmas. Howard was never comfortable with a tree in the house. Therefore, he is happy that Christmas is leaving our home. As I said before, my children will never know.

They will never know what it feels like to walk through the cold mud and snow searching for the perfect tree; they will never hear their father angry because the tree is too large for the stand; they will never learn the art of watering the tree without getting any of the gifts wet.

They will never know the feeling of getting the boxes of decorations out of the attic. They will never know the fun and joys of decorating a tree. They will never tell stories about each precious ornament. They will never sing carols in front of a roaring fire while they trim the tree. My children will never feel the dismay that comes when the tree falls over. They will never know the feeling of being a teenager in love in front of the fire and the tree. They will never know the joys of watching for Santa Claus, or recount the story of when Santa knocked on the window and told them to go to bed.

My children will never leave out cookies and milk for Santa; They will never feel the peace of sitting by the fire with Christmas lights on and carols playing softly in the background. My children will always think of December 24 as my birthday and not Christmas Eve. They probably will not know that my middle name is Carol for a Christmas Carol and that my mother wanted to name me Noel.

My children will never know the sweet smell of pine as they walk into our home. My children will never know the special feeling that the season generates. My children will never know Christmas. My children will not feel deprived because they will know the joys of being Jewish and the warmth and love that abounds in their family and their home. My children will never feel a loss. But I will.

How I long for the day when the loss of Christmas and my tree will not hurt so much. When my memories will be sweet memories instead of bittersweet.

Despite all of these emotions, the question of a tree or no tree is an easy one. The literature makes it clear that trees are not part of the Jewish religion. I am committed to being a Jew and that commitment means no tree. I can be thankful that as I mourn the loss of Christmas and cry for the loss, there are two big arms to hold me and to remind me that I haven't lost Christmas. I've found a new and beautiful way of life.

* * * * * * * * * *

The following questions may be used to spark discussion:

1. What was your reaction to this essay?

2. The author articulates a feeling of personal loss connected to letting go of something very special from her past. While she is reconciling herself to this loss, she understands that her children's point of reference is totally Jewish and that they do not share her past or her sense of loss. Describe the loss you think she is feeling.

3. The author represents a significant population of members of our congregations. What do we learn from this statement about making the transition to Jewish life?

4. How does this essay sensitize us to some of the experiences of the Jew-by-Choice? What does it bring to light about your negative and/or positive feelings about Jews-by-Choice? How does knowing how the author feels about Christmas affect the way we feel about her?

5. How can we become involved in the process of welcoming new Jews-by-Choice and their families into the community?

6. What Jewish traditions would you find hard to give up?

PROGRAM 3E

Title: Religion and Family

Objectives:
1. To provide an opportunity for participants to talk with one another about religion and family in a safe environment
2. To help participants consider how families change over time in relation to religion and religious behavior

Time Required: One hour

Materials Needed: Blackboard and chalk

Instructions for the Facilitator:

1. Write discussion questions on the blackboard.

2. Divide into groups of four. Each group should choose a facilitator who will be responsible for keeping time and ensuring that each person has a chance to speak. (The facilitator speaks as well.)

3. Instruct group members to talk with one another for 15-20 minutes about the following topics:

    * What do you remember about the religious behavior of your grandparents?

    * What do you remember about the religious behavior of your parents?

    * Discuss your own religious behavior;

    * How do you imagine your children will behave religiously as adults?

    Note: Religious behavior should be defined very broadly. It does not refer exclusively to ritual practice. Examples need not be Jewish since there may be participants who have parents and/or grandparents who are Jews-by-Choice or non-Jews.

4. Stop discussion and direct groups to conclude by considering the following question, allowing several minutes for discussion.

    * Were there any common themes reflected in the discussion?

5. Reassemble the group. Now that you have discussed the personal Jewish history of your grandparents, parents and selves, we can consider the following:

   * How has religious practice differed in the various generations?

   * What are the threads that tie the generations together?

   * How and when might personal family history affect you in some way in the future?

   * What events in life might cause us to be "pulled back" to our family tradition?

   * In an interfaith relationship, what might happen if we are not aware of the possibility of these "pulls?" How might this cause conflict?

   * How can understanding our personal religious/ethnic/cultural history prepare us to make decisions before or during a relationship?

   * As you grow older, your needs and expectations change. What might cause you to move away from or alienate you from your roots? What might pull you back?

6. Concluding remarks may include:

   * We understand ourselves in relation to our pasts;

   * We often assume previous generations were more religious than we are without adequately defining "religious behavior;"

   * There are different ways to be "religious;"

   * What are our expectations of ourselves in relation to religious behavior?

Adapted from: <u>Outreach and the Changing Reform Jewish Community: Creating an Agenda for Our Future</u> (UAHC, 1989). Reprinted with permission.

PROGRAM 3F

Title: Jewish Values And Beliefs: A Program For Teens and Their Parents

Objective: To open up channels of communication in families about Jewish values

Time Required: One and one-half hours

Materials Needed: A copy of the questionnaire for each participant, pencils

Instructions for the Facilitator:

1. Have each participant, teenager and adult, fill out the following questionnaire for him/herself. Participants should put their personal responses in the "MY VIEW" column, and they should guess at their parent's or child's responses in the "THEIR VIEW" column.

2. Parents and teenagers then discuss the questions, comparing predicted with actual responses. If responses differed, discuss these differences and what might be the cause of this communication gap. If they agree, how did family members learn about the others' views? Focus on issues about relationships, communication of values, views of religion, intermarriage, God, and education.

   The optimal size of a group is 10-15 participants. Groups can be divided as follows: teens and parents mixed, with teens in different groups from their parents; or teens together with their parents in groups run by facilitators trained in group skills. It is important to be sensitive to the fact that in some cases a parent may not be present and this may make the teen uncomfortable.

3. A group facilitator can bring the small groups together to share findings. This can lead to discussions on how parents or teenagers in general responded to specific issues, or why areas of concern differed from one family to another. Care should be taken to ensure that no family is made to feel defensive in front of the group. Remember that parents may be Jews-by-Choice or non-Jews and, in the case of some blended families, some of the children may not be Jewish.

QUESTIONNAIRE ON JEWISH VIEWS AND BELIEFS

Fill out the following questionnaire. Put your personal responses in the "MY VIEW" column. Indicate in the "THEIR VIEW" column what you think your parent's or child's responses might be.
(Use a scale of 1-5: 1 is Agree, 3 is Neutral, 5 is Disagree)

		MY VIEW	THEIR VIEW
1.	Children ought to accept the same religious beliefs as their parents.		
2.	Respect between parents and children must be earned reciprocally.		
3.	Celebrating Jewish holidays together is a responsibility all family members should accept.		
4.	Organized religion is old-fashioned and basically of no help in leading a better life in the real world.		
5.	Jews should only marry other Jews.		
6.	Judaism is no better or worse than other religions.		
7.	Jews should support all charities equally, Jewish and non-Jewish.		
8.	Jews should try to be similar to other Americans.		
9.	It is a good idea for Jews to have mostly Jewish friends.		
10.	God has little meaning for educated people.		
11.	A Jewish education is as important as a secular education.		
12.	Jews should have a special loyalty to the State of Israel.		
13.	Anti-Semitism is no longer a real problem in America.		

Excerpted from: "Celebrating Together: Joint Programming for the Temple Youth Group and Sisterhood." Published by NFTS Women of Reform Judaism, 1989. Reprinted with permission.

PROGRAM 3G

Title: Exploring the Jewish Community

Objectives:
1. To acquaint participants with the range of institutions that make up the fabric of Jewish life.

2. To sensitize participants to their own perceptions or biases based on experiences with Jewish institutions.

3. To provide participants with a perspective on issues that arise when individuals and institutions interface.

4. To enable participants to understand that Outreach issues related to Jewish institutions are complex as a result of objectives 1, 2 and 3.

Time Required: One hour

Materials Needed: Pencils and paper

Instructions for Facilitators:

1. Taking just five minutes, ask the group to list Jewish institutions and organizations, which the facilitator should write on a blackboard. The range should be as broad as possible and may include:

    United Jewish Appeal
    synagogues
    YMHA/YWHA
    Federation
    UAHC
    CCAR
    HUC-JIR
    ARZA
    Mazon
    Jewish camps
    NFTY, TYG
    National Council of Jewish Women
    B'nai B'rith
    Hadassah
    Jewish Schools

2. Ask participants to choose a partner whom they do not know well. Allow <u>15 minutes</u> for each partner to tell about <u>either</u> a <u>best</u> personal experience with a Jewish institution or organization or a <u>worst</u> personal experience with a Jewish institution or organization. The experience need not be recent.

3. Reconvene the large group. Ask for a show of hands to ascertain how many people chose to discuss a <u>best</u> experience, and how many chose to discuss a <u>worst</u> experience. If the group is weighted one way or the other, ask the group any of the following questions:

   * Why do institutions exist?

   * Why do you think so many people reported negative experiences? Positive experiences?

   * What group pressures might be operating to focus on the positive, since this program is sponsored by a Jewish institution?

   * Do you think that your choices are representative of the Jewish community as a whole? Why? Why not?

4. Ask for volunteers to tell the large group <u>very briefly</u> about the experience they discussed. (You will need to be assertive in moving the participants along with their stories.) Ask for positive experiences first, permitting 4 or 5 people to speak. Repeat for negative experiences.

5. Discuss: One important aspect of being Jewish is being part of a group - a community.

   a. What reactions does the group have to the stories just presented?

   b. What are your positive, negative and/or ambivalent attitudes toward the Jewish community?

   c. What makes up our Jewish community? Institutions? People?

   d. Of course it is people who make our institutions "go." Why do we need the structured institutions?

   e. What might happen to Jewish life without our institutions?

   f. What are your expectations from the Jewish organizations you are associated with?

   g. Do they meet your expectations?

   h. Do you even know how to define your own expectations?

i. How can you begin to understand your own Jewish feelings and needs?

j. What can you do to ensure that your needs are met by the organized Jewish community?

k. How do you see the future?

Note: Additional exercises can be found in <u>The Intermarriage Handbook: A Guide for Jews and Christians</u> by Judy Petsonk and Jim Remsen (Arbor House, 1988) pp. 105-106, 117.

PROGRAM 3H

Title: <u>Considering Stereotypes: A Workshop For Adolescents</u>

Objectives:
1. To enable participants to understand the nature of stereotyping and its effect on individuals and society.

2. To provide participants with an opportunity to consider how Jews have been stereotyped historically.

3. To help participants understand how they may have internalized stereotypes about Jews, especially stereotypes related to the opposite sex.

Time Required: Two to two and one-half hours

Materials Needed: Blackboard or large pad for <u>Part I</u>
Large pad or life-size piece of paper, masking tape, and assorted thick magic markers for <u>Part II</u>. (<u>Life-size paper works best</u>. You can also use the white side of a role of heavy gift wrap).

Instructions for the Facilitator:

<u>Part I</u>

Begin by explaining to the group that this workshop is related to stereotyping and its impact on individuals and society. Ask the group for a definition of the word "stereotype" and encourage discussion and grappling with the concept. You may want to explain that the term <u>stereotype</u> originally referred to a metal plate cast for printing which was used to make reproductions, each exactly like the last. Webster currently defines <u>stereotype</u> as "a standardized mental picture...that represents an oversimplified opinion. Lacking in originality or individuality." Thus, stereotypes are labels that do not take the individual into account.

To help participants understand the nature of stereotypes, write the following categories on the blackboard: Italian, Black, Polish, Oriental, and WASP. Ask for examples of prevailing stereotypes about each group and write responses under the appropriate heading. Note that you are <u>not</u> asking participants to indicate how <u>they</u> feel about these groups, but instead simply to recall stereotypes they've heard, even if some of them are uncomfortable to repeat. Be sure to provide ample time. Reassure participants that the goal is to label stereotypes and consider their accuracy.

(Typical responses for Poles may include: dumb, poor English, heavy drinkers, etc; for Italians: connected to the Mafia, gluttony, greasy, always happy, etc.; for Blacks: great athletes, natural rhythm, lazy, shiftless, etc.; for Orientals: smart, over-achieving, technologically oriented, etc.; for WASPS: snooty, wealthy, conservative, intolerant, etc.)

Discuss the answers generated by your group. Were most of the entries positive or negative? Were stereotypes of some groups more negative than others? Was it difficult to begin the exercise and write some of the stereotypes on the board? Why or why not? Ask the group to imagine that Black, Italian, Polish, Oriental, and WASP teenagers were present. Would it be easier or harder to do the exercise? Why? (While stereotypes about many groups are rampant, we see them as generally inaccurate and reflective of prejudice. They reflect the views and feelings of outside groups and are not reliable descriptions.)

The facilitator should summarize by stating that while some stereotypes may be positive, the majority are negative and reflect prejudice. STEREOTYPES REFLECT THE INSECURITY OF THE GROUP WHICH ASSIGNS THEM. (If Group A is stereotyped negatively by Group B, then Group B is able to feel better about itself by comparison.)

Finally, ask the group to think about individuals they know who belong to each of the groups listed. Does every stereotype on the list apply to that person? (Don't encourage discussion of specific individuals.) Does that person have characteristics which are not included on the list of stereotypes? Why aren't those qualities included in the list? (The goal of this discussion is to help participants to recognize that, for the most part, stereotypes are inaccurate or overgeneralized.)

Part II

Explain to the group that you now want to broaden the consideration of stereotypes to include Jews. Participants will break up into a male group and a female group. The task of each will be to illuminate stereotypes about the other. You will need an adult facilitator for each group.

The facilitator of each group explains that the task at hand is to create a stereotype of Jews of the opposite sex. Ask the group to come up with a name for the stereotype they are about to bring to life. (i.e. the boys' group will need a name for a Jewish girl, while the girls' group will need a name for the Jewish boy. Be sure to ask how the name should be spelled. Remember that the group's choice of a name may reflect a stereotype in itself.) Ask for a volunteer to draw a picture of the group's stereotype on the pad or large paper as he/she is described. (The volunteer need not be an artist). As the picture is completed, list the stereotypes that arise in discussion on the paper next to the picture. Encourage the group to be creative and outrageous.

The facilitator guides the group in describing the stereotype to be drawn on the large paper or pad in the following manner:

For determining stereotypes of Jewish girls/women: "Let's being to draw our picture of "Cyndi". We'll start with her head: What does her hair look like? What color? What style? What does it say about her? How about her face...Is she wearing make-up? How much? What do her eyes look like? Her nose? Mouth? Let's draw a cartoonist bubble coming out of her mouth -- What is she saying? What is she wearing? Is it like the other kids' clothing? Why/Why not? Where did she buy it? Is she wearing jewelry? What? How much? etc."

When the picture is completed, ask the group to "anchor" it to a background. What is "Cyndi" doing? What would they like to put in her hand? Next to her?

Finally, tell the group that this is to be a picture of "Cyndi" that will be used for the school yearbook. Write a brief description of her for the caption.

When the exercise is completed, ask for a volunteer or pair of volunteers to introduce "Cyndi" to the girls when the groups reconvene. They will need to bring the picture, tape it up, and explain it, noting the list of stereotypes which have evolved in their discussion.

The procedure for the girls' group is similar. They are to create a stereotyped caricature of a Jewish boy. Describe him from head to toe, and remember to add the cartoon bubble coming out of his mouth. Put him in context by anchoring him to a background. Complete the caption for the yearbook. Be sure to get a volunteer to introduce him when the groups reconvene.

(This may be an appropriate time for the group to take a break. Instruct participants that they are not to discuss the exercise with the other group during the break. They will have ample opportunity when they reconvene.)

Part III

When the groups reconvene, give each group an opportunity to introduce its drawing to the others and describe it completely. Highlight stereotypes that arose in discussion and be certain to read the yearbook caption. Encourage reaction, discussion, and debate.

After each group has had an opportunity to present their drawing and time has been allotted for discussion, ask the group to consider how the stereotypes they identified are reflected in an historical context. It would be useful to have on hand copies of Nazi racist cartoons, a photograph of Woody Allen as the stereotypical Jewish nebbish, a copy of the JAP Handbook, and/or any other examples of historical or contemporary Jewish stereotypes.

Be sure to take time at this point to ask participants what the experience of the workshop was like for them. Were they nervous about labelling other groups? Each other? Did the other group listen? Note that defensive reactions are appropriate: none of us likes to be described by externally imposed labels.

The workshop is completed with concluding remarks by the facilitator which should include the following:

1. The stereotypes each group created reflected, at least in part, both historical and contemporary prejudice toward Jews.

2. Note that the real tragedy about prejudice is that the group being stereotyped is likely to internalize society's prejudice about them. This is known as "identifying with the oppressor." Victims of prejudice also tend to project negative stereotypes about their ethnic group onto members of the opposite sex. Thus Jewish men may, on some level, perceive Jewish women as JAPS, while Jewish women may believe Jewish men to be Mama's boys, etc. Finally, members of the opposite sex may actually be seen as the enemy: Jewish men don't want to be dominated by "pushy, demanding JAPS," while Jewish women may see Jewish men as "impotent nebbishes and nerds" to be avoided at all costs. This process has grave implications for our Jewish future: dating and mate-choice may be disrupted, and we become our own worst enemies.

3. Conclude by stating that the kinds of stereotypes that have been described during the workshop have evolved over thousands of years. The way we have internalized those stereotypes will not be changed overnight. While it is not comfortable to address the issues raised in the workshop (refer to the reluctance to label other groups in <u>Part I</u>, nervous laughter at various points during the workshop, etc.), recognizing our stereotypes of one another is the beginning of healing. Remind participants that in all aspects of our lives we do not relate to one-dimensional paper drawings, but to real people who deserve to be treated as individuals instead of as caricatures created by a xenophobic society.

PROGRAM 3I

Title: Choosing to be Jewish

Objectives:
1. To enable participants to begin to understand the range and complexity of the Jewish choices in an individual's identification with Judaism.

2. To enable participants to see a connection between the Jewish choices they make and the choices made by Jews-by-Choice.

3. To expose participants to perspectives different from their own.

Time Required: Twenty to thirty minutes, if used as a focusing exercise (longer if used as a program)

Materials Needed: Copies of the exercise, pens and pencils

Instructions for Facilitator:

1. Hand out the exercise, instructing participants not to begin reading the worksheet until they are instructed to do so.

2. Assure participants that this is an anonymous, fill-in-the-blank exercise whose goal is to help the group focus on choosing how to be Jewish. They should write whatever first comes into their minds. There are no right or wrong answers. They must work quickly, since they will only be given three minutes to complete the exercise.

3. Instruct the group to begin, and time the exercise for three minutes. If, at the end of three minutes, many people are still writing, allow another minute or two for the group to complete the exercise. Collect the papers.

4. Ask for reactions to the content or to having to focus their thoughts on the topic under pressure.

5. Choose 4-5 sentences which are most appropriate for your discussion. Read aloud one sentence at a time, filling in the blanks with answers from the participants' papers. Encourage reactions/discussion.

    Imagine you are someone who is considering becoming Jewish and are asking these questions. How would you feel in being presented with such a variety of responses?

6. Summarize, possibly commenting on: the range of response, points of agreement or disagreement, complexity of the issues, need to focus on specific parts of a very large topic, participants' difficulty in completing specific statements, etc.

Fill in the blanks with the first thing that comes into your mind. Remember, there are no right or wrong answers! If you get stuck, move on to the next question and go back when you are finished.

1. I am a Jew who_____.

2. The single most important ingredient in establishing a strong sense of Jewish identity is _____
_____.

3. The most negative aspect of contemporary Jewish life is ____
_____.

4. _____should be a part of every American Jew's life.

5. Belief a God is _____to the Jewish future.

6. You don't have to _____to be a good Jew.

7. The most fulfilling part of my own Jewish identity is _____
_____.

8. If I were honest, I would admit that the part of my Jewishness that I feel most insecure about is_____
_____.

9. The best reason to convert to Judaism is _____
_____.

10. Becoming a Jew-by-Choice should require _____
_____.

11. I think intermarriage _____.

PROGRAM 3J

Title: Being Jewish: A Values Clarification Program

Objective: To help teenagers focus on personal aspects of Jewish identity

Time Required: One hour

Materials Needed: One copy of the exercise for each participant, pencils

Instructions for the Facilitator:

Hand out copies of the exercise, instructing participants not to look at it until you tell them to begin.

Emphasize the following:

1. There are no right or wrong answers.

2. Answers are anonymous. Participants are not to put their names on the sheet.

Tell participants that they have only two minutes to complete the exercise, so they should fill in the blanks with the first thing that comes to mind. Note when one minute has elapsed so they will continue to work quickly. When the time is up, you may allow up to another minute if most participants are still writing.

Collect the papers, shuffling them to insure anonymity. Compare and discuss participants' answers to selected questions, noting the range of responses, consensus, disagreement, etc. Not everyone connects with their religion in the same way at the same time.

Fill in the blanks with the first thing that comes into your mind. Remember, there are no right or wrong answers! If you get stuck, move on to the next item and go back when you are finished.

1. I feel most Jewish when I _____.

2. Deep down, my parents really think that religion _____.

3. My Jewish friends _____.

4. When I think about my future, my involvement with Judaism will probably _____.

5. To be a good Jew, a person should _____.

6. The hardest thing about being Jewish is _____.

7. The best part of my Jewish education was _____.

8. I wish that adults would understand that for most teenagers religion _____.

9. I felt most connected to my religion when _____.

10. The Jewish experience I look forward to most is _____.

11. I became aware of anti-Semitism when _____.

12. The most important thing Judaism has taught me is _____.

13. I feel badly about Jews who think that Judaism _____.

SECTION TWO

PART FOUR

PROGRAMS USING HISTORICAL PERSPECTIVES AND TEXT STUDIES

PROGRAM 4A

Title: Attitudes in Transition: Exploring Jewish Identity Through the Use of Jewish Texts

Objective: To provide participants with source material from Jewish tradition which offers a conceptual framework for the discussion of Jewish identity and conversion

Time Required: The length of the program will depend on how many of the quotations you choose for discussion. Plan a minimum of an hour and a half.

Materials Needed: Copies of the source material for each participant; pencils and pens

Instructions for the Facilitator:

Texts have much to teach us. They are verbal artifacts. Reading them, we gain clues to secrets of human knowledge and behavior. Exploring them, we learn about the beliefs and attitudes of others. We measure our attitudes against them; we expand what we know. Texts allow us to travel beyond the boundaries of our own experience and our own time and place.

The material to be handed out includes:

- classical texts which show us what Jewish tradition says about Jews-by-Choice and Jewish identity;

- poetry which, in its compression, is perhaps the best expression of the complexities of the human psyche. As we examine the words and images, we gain a deeper understanding of how human beings struggle with feelings which may sometimes contradict one another.

We hope that you will study and discuss these texts. By looking deeply into these words, we look deeply into our own hearts.

In order for this material to be meaningful to teenagers, the program should be active and include the participants in the process of discussion, debate or problem-solving. Consider using the material as a homework assignment to be read before the Outreach videotape on conversion, "Choosing Judaism: Some Personal Perspectives." This 30-minute video cassette, discussion guide included, is available in VHS or BETA format for $35 from the UAHC TV and Film Institute, 838 Fifth Avenue, New York, NY 10021.

You might also consider distributing the "Helen McDonald" exercise (attached) and asking participants, in small groups, to look for source material that substantiates or refutes

87

their own responses to the exercise. Better yet, since you know your group best, write several scenarios of your own that will be appropriate for the group to use in relation to the sources presented.

Text: Beyond Conversion: Attitudes in Transition

I. <u>Classical Rabbinic Texts on Converts and Conversion</u>:
A sampling of classical Rabbinic attitudes toward the convert.

This period was between the first century through the first half of the sixth, when Christianity was born. Talmudic Judaism was the precursor of the Judaism of our own time.

The attitudes of the rabbis ranged from friendly to enthusiastic. Their motive for proselytizing was to fulfill the messianic vision of the world being one by worshipping the one God.

What should our attitude be about welcoming converts in an age of self-affirming minority groups, where ours is a vision of unity without uniformity? What is the effect of the Holocaust on our attitudes toward welcoming the Jew-by-Choice when Jewish survival has been placed on the agenda of human concern?

Various Christian scholars date the cessation of Jewish proselytizing from before the destruction of the Temple (70 CE) to the latter part of the second or early in the third century.

The Rabbinic literature tries to protect the self-esteem of the newcomer, even romanticizing his/her status in an attempt to create a climate where more converts could be attracted. ("The convert is more beloved to God than those who stood at Mt. Sinai.") There is no mistaking the rabbis' approval of proselytizing and their attempt to idealize Jews-by-Choice.

That is not to say we cannot find disparaging remarks in the literature: R. Helbo, a third century Amora, said that converts are troublesome as an itch. But scholars feel such comments reflect the political climate of repression at that time. The mainstream of Rabbinic law and ethics declares that there should be no restrictions in status or rights of those who have converted to Judaism.

Use some of the following selections to examine how we value Jews-by-Choice. Is our additude as laudatory as the mainstream of Rabbinic literature? If there is a difference, what accounts for it? Select one or two passages to serve as a <u>D'var Torah</u> at the beginning of a program.

1. You must not remind the proselyte of his pork-eating, idol-worshipping past. If he comes to study the Torah you must not say to him, "Shall the lips that gobbled forbidden foods and creeping abominations mouth the words of God?" Such verbal mockery is worse than dishonesty in business. It is comparable to the worship of idols. Wounding the feelings of a proselyte or oppressing him involves transgression of three negative injunctions. If you ridicule him he has every right to come back with: "You, too, were a stranger in the land of Egypt." Reproach not your fellow with your own fault. The older proselyte is especially enjoined to treat the newcomer kindly inasmuch as he knows the soul of the stranger. Should a proselyte be in financial difficulties the Jew is required to help him, even to anticipate his difficulties.
   -Mekilta

2. R. Simon B. Lakish, a third century Palestinian Amora warns a judge who may be prejudiced against proselytes. He declares, "He who perverts justice against a proselyte is deemed as though he had turned against God himself." The same Amora permits Jews to buy slaves at a fair of heathens, for thus they can bring them under the wings of the Shechinah. The heathen slave acquired by a Jew is circumcised, taken to the Mikveh and consequently included within certain limits of Jewish law, such as the observance of the Sabbath.
   -Mekilta d'R. Simon

3. There is a tradition that after the serpent had beguiled Eve, moral taint settled upon her and her descendants. It was removed from the children of Israel when they received the Torah at Mount Sinai. But what of the proselytes who had not been there? R. Ashi answered: Even though they had not been there in the flesh their stars were present. For it is said, "But with him that standeth here with us this day before the Lord our God, and also with him that is not here with us this day."   (Deut. 29:14)
   -Shabbat 145b-146b

4. "Towards the righteous and the pious, towards the elders of Thy people the house of Israel, towards the remnant of their scribes, towards the proselytes of righteousness, and towards us also may Thy tender mercies be stirred, O Lord, our God..."
   -Amidah, Daily Prayerbook

5. At the time the children of Israel were exiled, the ministering angels protested to God: "Master of the Universe, when the children of Israel dwelt in their own land, they attached themselves to idols of gold and silver. And now that You disperse them among the nations they will abandon You altogether." But God answered them: "I know that My children will not abandon Me; nay more they will be My martyrs. They will offer their very lives to bring others under My wings."
   -Pesikta Rabbati

6. In the eulogy spoken by R. Simon B. Lakish, a third century Palestinian Amora, for his pupil R. Hiyya B. Ada. The preacher based his homily on the text, "My beloved is gone down to his garden, to the best of spices to feed in the gardens, and to gather lilies. (Canticles 6.2) "My beloved," is the Holy One of Blessing. The world is "His garden." As for "the lilies," they are the righteous whom He removes unto Himself. This is like unto a king who had a dearly beloved son. In his great love for him, he planted a beautiful orchard and bestowed it upon him. When the son obeyed his father, the latter traversed the breadth of the earth to find lovely trees and transplant them into his son's orchard. But when the son was disobedient the father would cut down the trees of the orchard. So, too, when Israel does the will of the Holy One of Blessing, God traverses the earth, and wherever God finds a righteous man, God attaches him unto Israel. Even so God did with Jethro and Rahab. But, when the children of Israel provoke God, the Holy One removes the righteous from their midst."

-Shir Hashirim Rabbah

7. How are converts accepted by God?

God loves converts exceedingly. To what is this matter compared? To a king who had a flock. Once, a stag entered the flock; he went with the goats and grazed with them. When the flock came in to rest, the stag came in with them. The king was told. The king liked the stag. The king ordered: When the stag is in the field, let him have a nice shepherd; let no one harm him; be careful with him. When the stag comes in with the flock, given him something to drink. The shepherd said to the king: Master, you have so many male goats, and so many lambs and you don't warn us about them. Yet, concerning the stag you warn us every day. The king said to him: The flock has no choice, for it is their nature to graze in the field all day and come in each night to sleep in the stable. Stags, however sleep in the wilderness. It is not their nature to enter the living places of human beings. Shall we not consider it a merit for this one who has left behind all the vast wilderness, the place of all wild animals, and has come and stood in the yard? (Bamidbar Rabbah 8:2)

Similarly, shouldn't we be grateful to the convert who has left a family and a father's house and a people and all other peoples of the earth, and comes to us? Therefore, (God) provided extra protection, for God warned Israel that they should be careful not to harm them. And thus Scripture says: "You shall love the convert" (Deuteronomy 10:19).
Based on this passage, how should we respond to someone interested in conversion?

8. R. Simeon B. Eleazar said: I will expound this to you with a parable. To what might Adam be compared? To a man who married a proselyte and used to give her instruction, saying, "My dear, do not eat bread when your hands are defiled, do not eat untithed produce, do not profane the Sabbath, do not make vows rashly, and do not associate with another man. If you break one of these rules, you will die." Now what did a certain man do? He arose and ate in her presence bread although his hands were defiled, he ate before her untithed produce - he profaned the Sabbath and made vows rashly - and also offered her some (of the food). What could that proselyte have thought to herself? All that my husband forbade me in the beginning was without foundation. She there-upon went and transgressed them all.
   -Abot d'R. Nathan

9. Dearer to God than all of the Israelites who stood at Mt. Sinai is the convert. Had the Israelites not witnessed the lightning, thunder, quaking mountain, and sounding trumpets they would not have accepted the Torah. But the convert who did not see nor hear any of these things, came and surrendered himself to God and took the yoke of heaven upon himself. Can anyone be dearer to God than such a person?
   -Tanchuma Buber,
   Lech Lecha 6,32a

10. How shall converts be received?

    Those who seek to become converts because of their love for a Jew are not received. Neither are those who seek to become Jewish out of fear or because of some advantage. But Rav said: They are to be received. This is the law: They are to be welcomed immediately. They are not to be repelled at the beginning; and they must be treated kindly for perhaps they will become converts with pure intent.
    -Jerusalem Talmud;
    Kiddushin iv:i, 65b

11. The proselytes who studies the LAw counts as much as a High Priest.
    -Tanhuma

12. The proselytes who rest in the shadow of God becomes roots like Israel.
    -Vayikra Rabbah

13. "The Holy One of Blessing said: The names of proselytes are beloved unto me like the wine of libation brought upon the altar."
    -Vayikra Rabbah

14. Not all passages from Rabbinic literature are positive and welcoming.

> Ruth Zutra 1:12 reads: "Do not trust a convert even to the 24th generation, because the inherent evil is still within him." And, several times in the Talmud we find: "Converts are as hard for Israel as a sore."
> —Yebamot 109b, Kiddushin 70b

II. <u>Sampling of Classical Judaism's attitude toward conversion.</u> What do these passages indicate concerning the Rabbis' attitude regarding the status of proselytes and concern for their well being?

1. Abraham was forty-eight years old when he came to know his Creator. Yet he was not commanded to circumcise himself at that time and waited till he reached the age of ninety-nine (Gen. 17.24), in order not to shut the door in the face of proselytes, however advanced in years.
   —Bereshit Rabbah

2. Every Jew should endeavor to bring people under the wings of the Shechinah even as Abraham did.
   —Bereshit Rabbah

3. The Torah was given in public, openly, in a free place. Had it been given in the land of Israel, the Israelites could have said to the nations of the world, "You have no share in it." But since it was given in the wilderness, in a place free for all, everyone wishing to accept it could come and do so.
   —Mekilta

   It was given in the third month, in Sivan, under the constellation of Gemini (Twins) as a reminder to the children of Esau, Jacob's twin brother, that they were welcome to repent and to become Jews.
   —Pesikta d'R. Kahana

   Then, too, the covenant made at Sinai included proselytes of later generations. They also were adjured at that moment.
   —Shavuot 39A

4. Before the covenant with Israel had been made, God went around among the nations of the earth in a vain effort to persuade them to accept the Torah.
   —Sifre on Deut.

Despite this initial refusal God persisted in the hope that they would see the error of their ways. Hence God gave the Torah in four languages, and its syllables of revelation came from the four quarters of the earth.
-Midrash Tannaim

It was all part of an effort to imbue the gentiles with its sacred words. Indeed many proselytes were attracted. "Many maidens have come to love thee," is interpreted to mean that many proselytes have come into Israel when they heard the doings of God.
-Shir HaShirim Rabbah

The quota of Israel can be extended indefinitely even as a bag of nuts can be stuffed with grains of mustard and sesame. Indeed so numerous were the newcomers in the fold that the heathen prophet Balaam was impelled to exclaim: "Who hath counted the dust of Jacob or numbered the stock of Israel?"
-Pesikta Rabbati

5. A Gentile who seeks conversion nowadays is asked: Why do you seek it? Do you not know that Jews are now sorrowful and oppressed, banished and in exile, and plagued with sufferings? If he answers,"I know", he is admitted.
-Talmud Yebamot

6. Proselytes are dearer to God than Jewish saints.
-Simeon b. Yohai,
Mishnat R. Eliezer

7. God scattered Israel among the nations for the sole purpose that proselytes should be numerous among them.
-Pesahim, 87b

8. You ask me if you are allowed to use the words of blessing: "Lord God and God of our fathers"..."you have brought us out of the land of Egypt"....Yes, you may say all of this in the prescribed order and not change it in the least. In the same way that every Jew-by-birth says prayers and blessings, you, too, may pray and bless.... Do not consider your origin as inferior. While we are the descendants of Abraham, Isaac, and Jacob, you derive from Him through whose word the world was created. ("Letter to Obadiah the Proselyte," in *A Maimonides Reader* by Twersky, pp. 475ff.).

In response to a convert who was ridiculed by his teacher, Rambam also wrote: "He called you a fool? Astounding! A man who has left his mother and father, his birthplace, his country and its power, and attached himself to this lowly, despised, and enslaved people, who recognized the truth and righteousness of this people's Law, and cast the things of this world from his heart -shall such a one be called a fool? God forbid!" ("Letter to an Inquirer," Twersky, A Maimonides Reader, p. 477)

9. If the motives (of one who seeks to convert) are found to be acceptable, that person is told of the heaviness of the yoke of the Torah and how difficult it is for the average person to live up to the commandments of the Torah.

Even after completing the requirements for conversion, that person continues to be under suspicion until found worthy of respect by righteous behavior.

Despite these concerns, a convert is permitted to do everything a born Jew may do, except...when a congregation decides, before a worship service, that if a convert were to lead the service, the non-Jewish community would become upset, the convert may not lead the service. (Conversion to Judaism, D. Eichhorn, p.111).

10. Why be Jewish, today or any other? Because I prefer the side of the powerless to that of the oppressor. Because I agree with a religion that urges me to control my actions rather than my thoughts. Because I am proud to be associated with the Jews, who have coped for centuries with the modern problems of doubt, exile, and despair. Because I enjoy the warm, colorful fabric of Jewish life.

The Jewish civilization is like a splendid old tree on a windy plain. Age and weather have twisted its branches, thickened its bark, but its roots go deep and the twigs are green and alive. Under its shade, there is room for all. Being Jewish has given me no final answers, but I now have a place to take my questions, a way to live, and a people to travel beside me. What else could I want? (Sh'ma, a Journal of Jewish Responsibility, November 5, 1971).

Note: Additional text references can be found in The Talmudic Anthology, edited by Louis I. Newman, New York: Behrman House, Inc., 1978.

Excerpted from: Reform Jewish Outreach: The Idea Book, (UAHC, 1988). Reprinted with permission.

POETRY

These poems were written by Barbara Jackson during the time she was in the process of choosing to become a Jew. They are remarkable in the way they capture the process of decision, not by looking back on it, but by expressing the moment.

Note for the Facilitator: You may want to use the following discussion questions in conjunction with the poetry.

What relationships are being explored?

Has Ms. Jackson's involvement in the process of becoming a Jew changed from one poem to the next? How?

"Will this black memory shear my life?"
"How much has changed?"

These are stark questions about the change involved in becoming a Jew.

Who is being addressed?

Do these questions relate to one of the questions asked of new Jews-by-Choice during the conversion ceremony: "Have you given up your former faith and severed all other religious affiliation?

Ruth, the Biblical prototype of the Jew-by-Choice, left her home and family to go with her mother-in-law Naomi to the land of Israel to become a Jew. Must one sever all family ties to become a Jew?

Caitlin O'Sullivan, during her conversion ceremony, states: "I honor and thank my parents and my heritage for giving me life and the strength to commit myself to a belief that is my fulfillment, but different from theirs." In what way is this statement a resolution of the issues connected with family for new Jews-by-Choice?

* * *

My fear is not by day
It comes at night
In dreams of Jewish objects
And Catholic stained glass

In dreams I am a half-life
Part me, part Jew
My parents own these objects
And are impassive.

What? What? What meaning here?
These dreamy fingers sifting through my hair
A gesture so kind, but with those hands, so cold
If I go on, will this black memory shear my life?
God--I'll be there again, You know that
We'll fight some more, until You flee with the light
Then my lame mind will try to fit the pieces
As it limps down the road.

Lament
Let me erase your pain
You look at me as if my very sight
Injures your eyes
How much has changed?

This path I chose
Rates hatred in your eyes
A hard cold metal
I'm scared to touch

Hold me like before
I was young and hurt my knee
That was bad: you were there
This is good: where have you gone?

Ivri
My eyes were opened late to you
And now I learn what every child knows
Bringing to it an adult understanding.
Within the fields of Judaism
I am rested and at peace--
but strangely ill-at-ease, being a
Trespasser, peeping past the gates, wondering what
Passwords bid me enter.
This scared discomfort is like leaves upon the
Ground, covering the grass that blooms beneath.
If God is not worrying about my newness, my
Awkwardness, or the thick sound of Hebrew in my mouth,
Why should I?
These are such transient, shallow differences
Easily blown like leaves away, revealing what soon
Will grow to be a lasting oneness at the roots.

Barbara Jackson, Roslindale, MA

Ivri

1. My eyes <u>were opened</u> late to you
2. And now I know <u>what every child knows</u>
3. Bringing to it an <u>adult understanding</u>
4. Within the <u>fields of justice</u>
5. I am <u>rested and at peace</u>--
6. but <u>strangely ill-at-ease</u>, being a
7. <u>Trespasser</u>, peeping past the gates, wondering what
8. <u>Passwords bid me enter.</u>
9. This <u>sacred discomfort</u> is like leaves upon the
10. Ground, <u>covering the grass that blooms beneath</u>.
11. If <u>God</u> is not worrying about my newness, my
12. Awkwardness, or the <u>thick sound of Hebrew in my mouth</u>,
13. Why should I?
14. These are such <u>transient</u>, <u>shallow</u> differences
15. <u>Easily blown</u> like leaves away revealing what soon
16. <u>Will grow to be a lasting oneness at the root.</u>

Discussion Questions

1. Why does the author use "were opened" instead of "opened"?

2. What does "every child know?" Are we talking about intuition? Levels of Jewish knowledge? Familiarity with Jewish people, customs, etc.?

3. What is an "adult" understanding? Is the issue one of learning as opposed to perspective? How is this different from "what every child knows"?

4. What are the "fields of Judaism?" Why this metaphor?

5. Why is the language here so pastoral? Might this relate to the issue of conversion as a recognition of "authentic self," which promotes inner peace?

6. Why is she "strangely ill at ease?" What kinds of situations, issues, or encounters make Jews-by-Choice uncomfortable? Which make you uncomfortable?

7. "Trespasser" is a powerful word. Why is it used here?

8. What are the "passwords" of Judaism? Hebrew? Familiarity with culture or religion? Or something much more secret and intangible?

9. What do you think the fear ("scared discomfort") is about?

10. What is the "grass" she refers to? What do Jews-by-Choice have to offer the Jewish people that would be absent otherwise?

11. Why is the notion of God introduced here?

12. Why might Hebrew be a "thick sound?" Is the issue self-consciousness?

13. What happens emotionally with this line? Why does the tone change here?

14. How can we help ourselves and each other overcome such differences? What do Jews-by-Birth need to know about Jews-by-Choice?

15. What will blow Jews-by-Choice away?

16. How will this image of oneness, cohesiveness, and belonging come about?

Excerpted from: *Reform Jewish Outreach: The Idea Book*, (UAHC, 1988). Reprinted with permission.

IV. Title: "Helen McDonald"

Objective: To promote discussion and awareness of issues involved in the conversion process related to family and ambivalence

Time Required: One-half hour (longer if groups are large)

Materials Needed: Copies of the scenario for each participant

Instructions for the Facilitator:

Small group discussion or individual preparation are both effective ways of using this exercise. It is important not to let discussion degenerate into a consideration of whether rabbis should or should not officiate at intermarriages.

Scenario:

Helen McDonald has nearly completed the Introduction to Judaism course in her area and she and her fiance, Mel, plan to be married in several months. The rabbi will not officiate at intermarriages, so Helen must convert beforehand in order to be married by the rabbi. At this point, Helen is not sure that she is ready to convert: she is feeling nostalgic about Christmas and she is worried about what conversion will mean in relation to her family. Her parents, who are Catholic, have been unusually silent about her plans. Mel feels she should go through with the conversion even though she has doubts, so that they can be married by the rabbi. He has even offered to have a Christmas tree in their home to make her feel better. Mel's parents have just brought them a seder plate and a <u>Chanukiah</u> (Chanukah menorah) as engagement gifts. You are Helen's best friend.

<u>Discussion Questions</u>:

1. What would you advise Helen to do? Why?

2. Does this situation relate to something you have experienced? If so, how?

    How did you handle the situation?

Excerpted from: <u>Reform Jewish Outreach: The Idea Book</u>. (UAHC, 1988). Reprinted with permission.

PROGRAM 4B

Title: Jewish-Christian History: A Legacy of Pain

Objective: To provide background to help participants understand the historical antecedents to Jewish attitudes toward intermarriage

Time Required: Forty-five minutes to one hour

Materials Needed: Copies of the attached essay

Instructions for the Facilitator:

The attached article, reprinted from The Intermarriage Handbook, can be used most effectively if it is distributed to participants to read beforehand. It can be used as a homework assignment, as background for discussion at a retreat, or as material for a workshop. After participants have read the article, use the following guide for discussion.

Discussion Questions:

1. In The Intermarriage Handbook, the authors state that "History forms an invisible backdrop to every life decision." What does this statement mean?

2. Relating this statement to the implications of interdating and intermarriage, how will understanding the history of Jewish/Christian relations help you understand the reactions of your family and your community to interdating and intermarriage?

3. Why does the Jewish community react differently from the Christian community?

4. Do you ever think your parents' and grandparents' reactions are out of proportion to the situation?

5. Knowing the history, what are some of the emotional "pulls" one might feel when involved in an interfaith relationship?

6. Knowing that you are the first generation in 2000 years not to experience anti-Semitism on an organized political level, how might you look at interfaith relationships differently from your grandparents and parents?

7. What has Jewish tradition always maintained as being crucial to the survival of Judaism?

8. Why do Jewish people see intermarriage as a threat?

9. How do Jews see themselves in relation to Jewish/Christian history?

10. How does our response to question 9 affect our reaction to interdating and intermarriage?

11. What are some of the key conflicts between Jews and Christians during this 2000 year history?

12. What are the historical events that most recently shaped the attitudes of our grandparents and parents?

13. Why do these events still frighten American Jews today and influence their attitude toward the Christian community?

14. How was prewar Germany similar to America today?

<u>Summary and Closing Remarks:</u>
It is important to understand that though we are talking about a bitter history, Christianity did not exist merely to persecute Jews nor Judaism to deny the divinity of Christ. Each has a rich tradition. Familiarity with the historical context of intermarriage is critical to an accurate understanding of the concerns of the Jewish community.

JEWISH-CHRISTIAN HISTORY:
A Legacy of Pain

History forms an invisible backdrop to every life decision discussed in the pages of this book. You need to understand this history--a history of virulent Christian persecution of Jews--because it is bound to affect you in some way.

Jews see themselves through the lens of history as a people who have existed for nearly five thousand years. Most Jews are keenly aware, and most Christians are not, that for the last two thousand years Jews have suffered horribly and repeatedly at the hands of Christians. For many Jews, this history plays like a tape in the mind--a tape that is triggered by symbols such as a crucifix or a Christmas tree, and that repeats: "Crusades, Inquisition, pogroms, Holocaust."

Although young Jews today may never have experienced anti-Semitism, they are the first generation in two thousand years to have escaped it. In the 1930s, American Nazis were able to muster large anti-Jewish marches in the streets of New York City. In the 1950s and 1960s, some residential neighborhoods, private schools, hotels, and resort communities still excluded Jews. Even today we have talked with children who have heard the accusation "Christ-killer" from their Christian playmates.

We often talked to Christian partners (and even some assimilated Jews) who thought Jews were vastly oversensitive or paranoid about this history. Until you understand the viciousness and persistence of the persecution--its reappearance time after time after periods of apparent peace and amity--you cannot understand the reactions of Jewish relatives or the Jewish community to your intermarriage. Therefore we must begin on this gloomy but central topic. Seeing the accumulation of horrors, we hope, will help you to understand the "paranoia." Later we will be presenting many examples of couples who have overcome the barriers created by history. But in later chapters, when we allude to Jewish sensitivities, try to hear the tape playing that says, "Crusades, Inquisition, pogroms, Holocaust." Realize that your parents or in-laws are probably hearing it, too. This will set the psychological context for you.

Christianity began as a sect of Judaism. The first Christians were the apostles; they were all Jews who belonged to Jewish synagogues and abided by Jewish law. But when they began to proselytize among gentiles, they reached a momentous decision: Pagan converts would not be required to observe Jewish law. The early Christians believed that they were the logical evolution of Judaism, and that all Jews should and would join them. When that didn't happen,

"Jewish-Christian History: A Legacy of Pain" from The Intermarriage Handbook by Judy Petsonk and Jim Remsen, (c) 1988 by authors. Reprinted by permission of Arbor House (A Division of William Morrow & Co.)

a reaction set in that some historians have compared to the reaction of a child slamming the door on the parent's home. Christianity began to contrast itself to Judaism and to declare God's favor has passed from the "old" religion to the new (1).

Jews, for their part, saw the Christians as having betrayed and deserted the Jewish people--particularly after the Christians fled Jerusalem, refusing to join in an uprising against Roman rule. Some of the apostles were persecuted or killed. The style of the time was inflated rhetoric, and bitter words were exchanged. Unfortunately, this bitter rhetoric became part of the founding theology of Christianity and laid the groundwork for centuries of wholesale persecution of Jews by Christians. Some passages in the New Testament (particularly in the Gospel of John) were used by Church authorities to justify anti-Semitism, whether or not that was the Gospel writers' intent. The story of Jesus and the Pharisees, reiterated annually in the Easter liturgy, was used to inflame hatred of Jews.

In part, there was a political problem: In the early centuries of the Christian or Common Era, both Christianity and, to a lesser extent, Judaism were missionary religions competing for the same pagan populations. But there was also a theological problem. The early Christians had expected the imminent return of Jesus and the ushering in of the last days. When that didn't occur, they developed a new view: Jesus would return when all the world had come to believe in Him. According to Christian theology; the Jewish faith was destined to wither away and be replaced by Christianity.

But the Jews persisted as a separate people. They did not all flock to embrace Christianity. They were an embarrassment. And they came to be seen as an impediment to the uniting of the world under Christianity. Instead of being regarded as people who remained loyal, often against great odds, to their own precepts and way of life, they were seen by the Christian leadership as people who had defiantly rejected the Truth of Christianity.

Two ideas provided the theological justification for later Christian persecution of the Jews: The first, originated by Saint Justin (who lived from the year 100 to 165), said that Jews were ejected from Jerusalem and their land ravaged as divine punishment for the death of Jesus. Although crucifixion was a Roman punishment, abhorred by Jews, and Jesus in fact was executed by the Romans, the idea that Jews were Christ-killers and were collectively responsible for the death of Jesus became rooted in the Christian Church. While never an official part of church doctrine, neither was it officially repudiated until the Second Vatican Council (Vatican II) in the mid-1960's (2). The second doctrine, developed by Saint Augustine (354-430), said the Jews were kept alive by God much as Cain was kept alive after he murdered Abel--with a brand on his forehead. God had decreed that the Jews would be perpetual wanderers, serving as living proof of what happened to people who reject Christ. This doctrine was later used to justify forced conversions and mass expulsions of Jews from many countries.

The words hurled from the pulpit by early Christian leaders who became saints of the church are shocking to modern ears: In the fourth century Saint John Chrysostom, patron saint of preachers, who is particularly venerated in the Greek Orthodox church, delivered six sermons from the see (bishop's throne) of Antioch, in which he called Jews "the most miserable of all men, lustful, rapacious, greedy, perfidious bandits...they murder their offspring and immolate them to the devil." He charged that the synagogue is a house of prostitution and that Jews worship the devil. The Jews are guilty of deicide (killing God), he said, and there is "no expiation possible, no indulgence, no pardon." He said God hates the Jews and always hated the Jews. "He who can never love Christ enough will never have done fighting against those (Jews) who hate him" (3).

He was only one of many saints of the Christian church to unleash vituperation against the Jews.

When Christians succeeded in converting Emperor Constantine (306-337) and Christianity became the official religion of Rome, discrimination against Jews became standard practice throughout the empire.

The Church leaders and Christian rulers of the next few centuries were faced with what they saw as a dilemma (4). The teaching of Saint Augustine which so influenced this and later eras had two sides: Though Jews were destined to suffer, they were also destined to be preserved, as a witness people. Though extensive efforts could be made to persuade them to convert, they could not simply be exterminated or forced en masse to convert, as was done with pagan populations. At the same time, these Church leaders and rulers were very anxious to preserve Christianity's dominant position, and to make sure that neither Jews nor Judaism became attractive enough to lure Christians away from the faith.

Although both Church law and Roman law made it clear that Jews were not to be harmed, and that Judaism was to be tolerated, at the same time specific legislation severely restricted Jewish rights. Over the next three centuries, a series of laws were promulgated, sometimes by regional church councils, and sometimes by imperial Rome, which outlawed intermingling between Jews and Christians and which crippled Jews economically. Such legal restrictions continued to be enacted in various places through the sixteenth century. Although not all the laws were in effect at any one time or place, and there were periods in various parts of Christian Europe when Jews enjoyed acceptance, wealth, and even prominence, the net effect of these laws was drastically to undermine the status of Jews in the larger Christian society. As historian Raul Hilberg has pointed out, nearly every legal restriction placed on Jews by the Nazis echoed an earlier measure taken by a regional council or synod of the Church (5).

The Council of Elvira (Spain), 306, forbade Christians and Jews from marrying each other, having sexual intercourse, or eating together; by the following century, Jewish-Christian intermarriage was punishable by death. The Synod of Clermont, a region of France, in 535, and the Council of Toledo in Spain in 589 barred Jews from holding public office. The Synod of Orleans (France), in 538, and the Council of Toledo also prohibited Jews from employing Christian servants or owning Christian slaves. (Since agriculture and industry of the time were conducted through slave labor, this effectively prevented Jews from competing with their slave-owning Christian neighbors and they were driven out of agriculture and industry and restricted to small business and crafts.) Jews were barred from practicing law or becoming civil servants or officers in the army. The sixteenth council of Toledo in 693 ordered Jews to stop conducting businesses and to forfeit all land acquired from Christians.

Other measures were taken during this period directly to ensure that Judaism would always remain a minority religion vis-a-vis Christianity. Construction of new synagogues was prohibited and even repairs could not be made without permission. In 415, a synagogue built without permission was destroyed. In 425, the emperor abolished the traditional Jewish leadership, the patriarchate. It was a crime for Judaism to seek converts. Christians who converted to Judaism lost the right to their inheritance. (On the other side, the third Lateran Council in 1179 decreed that Jews could not cut off inheritance to a child who converted to Christianity.) And later the Synod of Mainz in 1310 defined conversion to Judaism by a Christian, or reversion to Judaism by a baptized Jew, as heresy, for which the punishment was burning at the stake.

The severity of the legislation varied from place to place, with Spain at certain periods being among the worst. In the mid-600s, in Spain, Jews were forced to sign an oath which, if followed, would make it impossible for them to practice their religion (6). Failure to keep the oath was punishable by burning or stoning. The Synod of Toledo, in 681, ordered the burning of the Talmud, the most important Jewish religious book after the Bible. The seventeenth council the following year banned all Jewish religious rituals and decreed that all Jewish children over the age of seven were to be taken away from their families and educated as Christians.

There were also Church-sponsored attempts to ridicule and humiliate the Jews and their religion. In Toulouse, France, for three hundred years from the mid-800s to 1160, each Good Friday a Jew was summoned to be publicly slapped by the bishop, symbolizing the belief that all Jews were responsible for the crucifixion of Jesus. Another custom, traces of which persisted until modern times was to make special mallets for a Holy Week ritual symbolizing the killing of Jews (7).

In various parts of Europe, Easter was a season not only of humiliation, but of danger. Clergy preaching against the Jews in Easter sermons would inflame the common folk, who would ravage the Jewish district, killing and burning. Easter riots continued in Eastern Europe down to the early 1900s (8).

Even though official Church teaching forbade forced conversion, periodically, local rulers allied with local clergy ordered entire Jewish communities to convert to Christianity under the threat of exile, confiscation of property, or death. In Spain in the seventh century, some ninety thousand Jews underwent forced conversion; the rest lost their homes and property and went into exile (9). Many brave Jewish souls suffered martyrdom or committed suicide rather than undergo forced conversion. Jews called this martyrdom Kiddush Ha-Shem--sanctification of the name of God.

Despite all the social and legal restrictions, in many places Jews and Christians continued to live in the same communities and to conduct business with each other. At certain times of the year, especially at Christian holidays, there would be threats and harassments, but between times, there would be relatively cordial interactions between neighbors.

But the situation for the Jews deteriorated dramatically after the year 1000. It was a time of turmoil for all Europe, and frequently the fear and frustration was taken out on Jewish bodies, Jewish homes, and synagogues. Many Christians had believed Jesus would reappear at the millennium. When the waited-for Second Coming did not occur, the Church was thrown into a crisis. Christianity sought a new direction. Muslims had captured Jerusalem and closed it to Christian pilgrims. In 1095, Pope Urban the Second called for the liberation of the Tomb of the Holy Sepulchre. Many of the faithful believed that this holy war was the beginning of the events that would culminate in the Second Coming. Thus began the Crusades--a three-hundred-year nightmare for the Jews. One reason many Jews cannot see the cross as a symbol of Christian love is that Crusaders marching beneath the banner of the cross massacred Jews by the thousands. During the first Crusade alone, Crusaders on their way to Palestine killed some five thousand Jews in the towns of Europe, then burned Jews alive in the synagogues of Jerusalem where they had taken refuge.

Some popes rebuked the Crusaders; many of the bishops and some of the nobility tried, with various degrees of effectiveness, to protect the Jews. Others, like Pope Innocent III (1198-1216), fanned the flames.

Prejudice, superstition, and a distorted version of church teaching fused into a generalized hysteria in which the Jews were seen as demons; in medieval art, they were depicted with horns and tails. In 1171, the Jews of Blois, France, were accused of ritual murder (using the blood of a child in their Passover matzoh), and thirty-three men, women, and children were burned at the stake. This slander was revived more than one hundred times in Western Europe as an excuse for executing Jews. The charge of ritual murder became a persistent part of the folklore of some parts of Christianity, with frequent trials through the eighteenth and nineteenth centuries in some parts of Europe. The most recent trial on this charge was held in Russia in 1911. The accusation even surfaced (to be quickly dismissed) in the United States in 1920 in Massens, New York (10).

In 1298, based on a rumor that Jews had desecrated the communion bread, or host, an army of Judenschachter (Jew-slaughterers) marched through Germany and Austria killing an estimated one hundred thousand Jews.

The hysteria against Jews intensified with the arrival of the bubonic plague. Jews were accused of poisoning the wells. In the 1300's, tens of thousands of European Jews were massacred on this charge. Religious fanatics--flagellants--though condemned by the Pope, roamed Germany and France, stirring up some of the attacks. Over two hundred Jewish communities were destroyed. Greed as much as fear triggered many of the charges. In some places, the Jews' belongings were parceled out to their accusers before they were even put on trial. In Strasbourg, on the basis of the poisoning charge, two thousand Jews were burned alive on a scaffold over a huge pit--in the Jewish cemetery, on the Sabbath. Their credit records were burned with them. The men died wrapped in their prayer shawls.

In the midst of all this chaos, Church councils continued to issue legislation restricting the rights and degrading the social position of the Jews. The Third Lateran (Roman) Council, convened by Pope Alexander III in 1179, banned Jews throughout Christian Europe from appearing in court as plaintiffs or witnesses against Christians. The Fourth Lateran Council, summoned by Pope Innocent III in 1215, made universal for all of Christian Europe a number of the restrictions that had been enacted earlier by regional synods. In addition, it added two particularly injurious laws. As had been required earlier of both Christians and Jews by one of the Muslim rulers, Jews would be required to wear distinctive clothing. (In some places, they had to wear badges, in others, pointed hats.) And the Council said that those who joined the Crusades would be absolved of their debts to Jews--a step which devastated the Jews economically. Moneylending was one of the major sources of income for some, since they were barred from many trades and industries. Ironically, this council, so devasting to Jews, was of profound theological importance to Christians. It was here that the doctrine of transubstantiation of the Communion wine and wafer was acclaimed and that the minimum religious duties of a Christian (annual confession and communion at Easter) were defined.

New legal restrictions continued to be announced by regional authorities. The Council of Bezier (France) in 1246 decreed that Christians who patronized Jewish doctors would be excommunicated. The Synod of Ofen (Switzerland) in 1279 prohibited Christians from selling or renting real estate to Jews. The Council of Basel in 1434, which like the Lateran was an ecumenical council applying to all of Christendom, barred Jews from getting academic degrees and from acting as agents in the conclusion of contracts between Christians.

Attacks on the Jewish religion also continued. The Synod of Vienna in 1267 prohibited Jews from arguing about religion with average Christians. Sometimes Jews were ordered to debate the relative merits of Judaism and Christianity--a debate whose outcome had already been decided. Following one debate (after the pope had called for an investigation of Jewish books) in 1240, in Paris, twenty-four cartloads of copies of the Talmud were burned (11). From the ninth century on, but particularly in the thirteenth century, Jews in various parts of Europe were compelled to attend sermons where Judaism was denigrated, Christianity extolled, and their conversion sought. In some places, their ears were inspected to be sure they weren't wearing ear plugs.

In the 1200s, the Inquisition began--the Church's tool to combat heresy. Although others were trapped in its coils, the most infamous of the Inquisitions, in Spain, was primarily directed at converts from Judaism--Conversos. The Spanish clergy and nobles--after forcing Jews to convert--doubted the authenticity of their faith. Despite the pope's objections to the conduct of the Inquisition in Spain, in one twelve-year period in the late 1400's, the Inquisition there burned at the stake thirteen thousand men and women who had converted to Christianity but were charged with secretly practicing Judaism.

In 1492, 170,000 Jews who would not accept Christianity were expelled from Spain. The voyage of Columbus was partly financed with their confiscated property. But even those who stayed and converted could not escape Christian fury. They were called Marranos (pigs). By limpieza (blood purity) statues, they were excluded from living in certain towns, and from public and religious offices, guilds, and colleges.

The Inquisition in Spain was not abolished until 1836.

During the late Middle Ages, an increasing number of cities adopted regulations forcing the Jews into ghettos. In some places these were simply quarters or sections of the cities. In other areas, they were walled compounds, locked from the outside, narrow areas crammed with people and prey to waves of plague and of fire. The Snod of Breslau, Poland, in 1267 and the General Council of Basel, Switzerland, in 1434 were among the earlier church councils to adopt policies of compulsory ghettoization; by the sixteenth century, they were common.

The Protestant Reformation called into question many Church practices, but not the theology of anti-Judaism. Martin Luther, frustrated in his initial attempts at friendly conversion of the Jews, called for the burning of synagogues "in order that God may see that we are Christians, and that we have not wittingly tolerated or approved of such public lying, cursing and blaspheming of His Son and His Christians "(12).

Exile was another result of the convergence of state power and Christian influence. Repeatedly, Jews were forced to leave homes where they had lived for generations, with nothing but the clothes on their backs. Sometimes the exile meant a lifetime of wandering and poverty, since many towns were closed to newcomers and many of the guilds which controlled the practice of crafts were closed to newcomers or to Jews. Christian society succeeded in creating the wandering Jew--the situation which Christian theology predicted. In the 1200s and 1300s, the Jews were expelled from England, France, and parts of Germany.

Many of the exiled Jews went to Eastern Europe, particularly Poland and Russia. They flourished for several centuries, but later it became apparent that in Eastern Europe, too, neither their religion, their property, nor their lives would be safe. From the early middle ages, through 1264, when they were given a charter of rights, to the mid-1600s, they were treated very favorably by the Polish kings. They eventually had their own parliament, with almost complete autonomy. They became traders and financiers, and were appointed tax collectors by the kings--a role which led to their undoing. From 1648 to 1667, there was an uprising of Eastern Orthodox Ukranian cossacks, in which thousands of the Roman Catholic Poles who dominated the region were killed. Jews, who served as middlemen between the Ukranian peasants and the Polish rulers, were the target of special fury. According to historians Margolis and Marx, some "victims were flayed and burned alive.... Infants were slit like fish or slaughtered at the breasts of their mothers or cast alive into wells. Women were ripped open and then sewed up again with live cats thrust into their bowels" (13). Some were given the option of forced baptism rather than death or torture.

Potok quotes a letter that seems to prefigure the Holocaust, describing the scene in one town where seven hundred Jews were killed: "Some were cut into pieces, others were ordered to dig graves into which Jewish women and children were thrown and buried alive" (14).

During this same century, Poland endured a series of invasions. Jews suffered from both ends of the invasions. First they were attacked by the invading Russians, Cossacks, and Swedes. When the invaders were repelled, they were attacked by the Poles, who claimed that they had collaborated with the invaders. By the time this bloody century was over, one fourth of the Jewish population of Poland had been murdered. Estimates of the deaths range from one hundred thousand to half a million.
Thousands of Jews wandered from town to town with no permanent home.

Russia was another major center of Jewish population. According to Chaim Potok, in 1850, there were 2,350,000 Jews living in Russia. Most were confined to a crowded region known as the Pale of Settlement. Once again, says Potok, the Jews were caught between an oppressed underclass (the peasants) and an oppressing ruling class (the noblemen), and became the target of blame and rage. There were frequent pogroms (violent mob attacks) and other difficulties for the Jews. The government added legal disabilities: economic restrictions, expulsion from villages and cities, forced conscription of young boys for twenty-five-year terms in the army, banning from academic schools, a special tax on the candles used by Jews for religious purposes. In the 1870s, the government removed many of the restrictions and there was a brief, enthusiastic flowering of Jewish culture--a mini-Renaissance. But then in 1881 Czar Alexander II was assassinated by a bomb. It was blamed on the Jews. There came a new wave of pogroms and restrictive legislation. The head of the Russian Orthodox Church, Konstantin Pobedonostev, announced his hope that "one-third of the Jews will convert, one-third will die and one-third will flee the country" (15).

Although this bitter history explains the suspicion and anger many Jews feel toward Christians or Christian religious institutions, it isn't the whole story. Just as many Christians are ignorant of how the Jews suffered at the hands of official and unofficial Christianity, on the other hand most Jews have an unfairly monolithic view of the relationship between Jews and Christians during the centuries of Christian hegemony in Europe.

There were both clergy and Christian rulers who attempted to protect the Jews and sometimes even to elevate them to positions of privilege and honor (16).

Pope Gregory the Great (540-604) forbade the bishops from intervening in internal Jewish affairs, prohibited forced conversions, and in cases where synagogues had been violated, ordered that they be returned to the Jews and restored to their former condition, or compensation paid. Other popes in the coming centuries followed this example. In fact, "disrupting Jews at worship" was an excommunicable offense. Many of the restrictions and expulsions were promulgated by secular rulers, often over the objections of Church officials.

There were also devoutly Christian rulers who treated the Jews fairly and had good relationships with them. The Frankish emperor Charlemagne employed a Jew as an ambassador. His son, Louis the Pious (814-840), granted letters of protection to Jews, permitted Jews to employ Christians, and instituted a large fine for the murder of Jews. Louis himself had a Jewish doctor.

The popes and many bishops consistently condemned the blood libel and well-poisoning charges.

Even when Christian leaders outlined a policy of discrimination against the Jews, they often set limits upon it. Saint Thomas Aquinas (1225-74) wrote that it was all right "to hold Jews, because of their crime, in perpetual servitude, and therefore the princes may regard the possessions of Jews as belonging to the state, however, they must use them with a certain moderation and not deprive Jews of things necessary to life" (17).

To understand the context in which the events described in this history occurred, it's also important to remember that the Europe of the Middle Ages was not made up of nation-states as we know them today, but was often splintered into small kingdoms and fiefdoms. For most of this period, neither popes nor emperors had real control over these many principalities, or even over the regional clergy, some of which enacted policies toward the Jews which were in conflict with the expressed wishes of the Church authorities in Rome.

If you are Jewish, the pogroms are the thing that most immediately shaped the attitudes of your grandparents' generation. Many of these grandparents lived through the pogroms or fled Europe to escape them. You may have heard a grandparent talk, for example, about the Kishinev pogrom of Easter Sunday, April 6, 1903, which left forty-nine Jews dead, five hundred injured and two thousand homeless.

The attitudes of Jews of your parents' generation were profoundly shaped by the Nazi Holocaust, in which six million Jews were killed. One of the most frightening aspects of the Holocaust to American Jews was that it originated in Germany, which, like America, was a place where Jews, to all outward appearances, were quite well integrated into society. Many American Jews cannot forget that there have been previous periods in Europe (in both Christian and Muslim Spain around the year 1000, for example) during which the Jews enjoyed social acceptance, prestige, wealth, and apparent security--only to find everything they had build smashed in a new round of persecutions.

Given the suffering Jews incurred at the hands of Christian Europe, apostasy--voluntary baptism or conversion to Christianity--was viewed as the ultimate betrayal of the Jewish people (18). Intermarriage to a Christian was seen as almost as bad. Most voluntary conversions to Christianity were looked upon as cynical opportunism--done not out of religious conviction but to escape the economic and social discrimination against Jews. Common people would spit three times when they met a voluntary apostate from Judaism, and would recite a verse from Isaiah, "Those who ravaged and ruined you shall leave you."

Although Jewish religious law holds that a born-Jew never loses his membership in the people, the vast majority of Jews until very recently regarded one who converted to Christianity as dead, irrevocably cut off from the Jewish community. Even today, most Jews view baptism as betrayal. Nearly all would say it is impossible to be Jewish and Christian at the same time.

Given the history of bloodshed and mutual suspicion, it is remarkable that we find ourselves where we are today. America itself has been a positive influence on Christian-Jewish relations. Jews found in America a more open society, free of many of the legal and social strictures that had so limited their options in Europe. In spite of the prejudices that erupted following the waves of immigration by Jews and other Europeans, they were gradually able to become assimilated into the larger society in a way that had never been possible in Europe. Especially since World War II, the relationship between Jews and Christians in the United States has changed dramatically. Jews have been economically successful, are socially respected and are seen as desirable marriage partners by many Christians.

The organized religions have changed markedly. As a result of the Holocaust, the Christian world has begun to come to grips with its history of anti-Semitism. Some Christian theologians and historians have called for a recognition of how Christian anti-Judaism laid the groundwork for the non-theological and Godless anti-Semitism of the Nazi era. Vatican II reassessed Catholic teachings about the Jews. The Church's new teachings state that Jews have a valid covenant with God which has never been revoked, and that an understanding of Judaism is essential for a valid Christian faith (19).

Most importantly, the declaration Nostra Aetate (In Our Time) specifically repudiated some of the most destructive ideas about Jews voiced by the Christian thinkers of earlier times. The Synod stated that although some Jewish leaders in Jesus' time may have pressed for His death, their actions "cannot be charged against all the Jews, with our distinction, then alive, nor against the Jews of today." The Synod added that "the Jews should not be presented (in Christian teaching or preaching) as rejected or accursed by God" (20).

Since the declaration, the Roman Catholic Church has undertaken a sweeping evaluation and revision of parochial school texts and curricula and retraining of teachers. The object is not only to root out negative references to the Jews, but to promote a positive understanding of Jewish culture and its contributions to Christian beginnings as well as to the world of today.

Protestant denominations have also taken steps responsibility for the redress some of the injuries done by Christians to Jews. The World Council of Churches (WCC) in 1948, five years after the end of World War II, while continuing to stress its intent to evangelize the Jews, stated that "Anti-Semitism is sin against God and man," and acknowledged that "churches in the past have helped to foster an image of Jews as the sole enemies of Christ, which has contributed to anti-Semitism in the secular world." The WCC called upon "all the churches we represent to denounce anti-Semitism, no matter what its origin, as absolutely irreconcilable with the profession and practice of the Christian faith" (21) In 1968, the WCC declared that the survival of the Jewish people in spite of all the efforts to destroy them makes it clear "that God has not abandoned them." In fact, said the declaration, the survival of the Jews is living proof that God also cares for those who do not believe in the divinity of Jesus (22).

There has also been a wave of scholarship and theology exploring Jesus as a Jew, and the Jewish roots both of his teachings and of many church practices.

Thus, those who attended Protestant or Catholic Sunday schools since the mid-1960s were taught a very different outlook on the Jews than was prevalent earlier.

In addition, both Protestant and Catholic Churches have made extensive efforts to develop mutually respectful contacts with Jews, through dialogue groups and other means. The Vatican, in setting up its Office of Catholic-Jewish Relations in 1969, stated that the dialogue must include "respect for the other as he is, for his faith and religious convictions. All intent of proselytizing and conversion is excluded" (23).

It is in this radically changed atmosphere that young Jews and Christians today are meeting and falling in love.

Although we have stressed Jewish-Christian relations in this chapter, those dealings were a minor theme for both religions during this two thousand-year span. Christianity did not exist merely to persecute Jews, nor Judaism merely to deny the divinity of Jesus. Both religions have their own grand and beautiful traditions that developed on their own terms along their own trajectories. These traditions offer much to sustain their members, as we make abundantly clear throughout this book.

But as life-affirming as Christianity can be, as full of goodwill to Jews as it now seeks to be, most Jews still feel the scars inflicted by the churches. Older Jews are generally either unaware of the changes in the outlooks of the churches or are skeptical: They may not believe that forty years of good relations between Judaism and Christianity are enough to ensure the definitive end of nearly twenty centuries of bad relationships. Thus, when intermarrying couples are considering such steps as a co-officiated wedding ceremony, or raising of their children in both Judaism and Christianity, they must appreciate the psychosocial residue of Jewish-Christian history. Many Jewish families will view their child's participation in any Christian ritual, or even entering a church, with horror and anguish. And the Jewish community in general will not accept attempts to fuse Jewish and Christian ritual or Jewish and Christian identity.

If you are Jewish, you may not feel an instinctive reflex against the church and its symbols. Or if you do, it may be something you want to "get past." But we aware that these feelings can return to you at unexpected moments and for unexpected reasons. Your family and members of the Jewish community quite likely will have the reflex. Remember that it is deeply grounded in a very real history.

NOTES

1. The history of early Christian-Jewish relations is from Father Edward H. Flannery, <u>The Anguish of the Jews</u>, New York: Macmillan, 1965, ch. 1-3. Euguene Fisher retells some of this material and gives perspective in <u>Homework for Christians: Preparing for Christian-Jewish Dialogue</u>, New York: National Conference of Christians and Jews, New York, 2nd rev. ed., 1986; and <u>Faith Without Prejudice: Rebuilding Christian Attitudes Toward Judaism</u>, New York: Paulist Press, 1977.

2. <u>Nostra Aetate</u> (Vatican II's reassessment of the relationship of Catholics to non-Catholics and non-Christian religions) is discussed by Fisher, <u>Faith</u>, pp. 23-26.

3. Flannery, <u>op</u>. <u>cit</u>., p. 48.

4. Our perspective on this period was shaped in part by an interview with Dr. Eugene J. Fisher, Director of the Secretariat for Catholic-Jewish Relations of the National Conference of Catholic Bishops, as well as by Flannery's book.

5. The summary of legal restrictions is from Raul Hilberg, <u>The Destruction of the European Jews</u>, Chicago: Quadrangle, 1961, pp. 5-6, as cited in A. Roy Eckardt, <u>Elder and Younger Brothers: The Encounter of Jews and Christians</u>, New York: Charles Scribner's Sons, 1967, pp. 12-14. Parts are also cited in Fisher, <u>Homework</u>, p. 27. We have supplemented this summary from Flannery, <u>op</u>. <u>cit</u>.

6. Flannery, <u>op</u>. <u>cit</u>., p.75.

7. Flannery, <u>op</u>. <u>cit</u>., p.85.

8. Except where noted otherwise, the history of the persecutions is largely condensed and paraphrased from Chaim Potok, <u>Wanderings: Chaim Potok's History of the Jews</u>, New York: Fawcett Crest, 1978, and from Flannery, <u>op</u>. <u>cit</u>. Some material also comes from Fisher, <u>Homework</u>.

9. From Fisher, <u>Homework</u>, p.16.

10. <u>Ibid</u>., p. 21.

11. *Ibid.*, p. 15. Even when the Jews won such a debate, it was at their peril. When the Jewish scholar Moses Nachmanides was ordered to debate Christian scholars before the king of Spain in 1263, the king declared Nachmanides' arguments more convincing. Within two years, the clergy succeeded in having him accused of blasphemy and exiled.

12. Potok, *op. cit.*, p. 435.

13. Max Leopold Margolis and Alexander Marx, <u>A History of the Jewish People</u>, New York: Harper & Row, 1965, p.552.

14. Potok, *op. cit.*, p. 445.

15. Potok, *op. cit.*, p. 499.

16. The history of Christian leaders who protected the Jews is largely from Flannery, *op. cit.*, and from the interview with Fisher.

17. <u>Letter to the Duchess of Brabant</u>, cited in Flannery, *op. cit.*, p.95.

18. <u>Encyclopedia Judaica</u>, Jersusalem: Keter Publishing (New York: Macmillan, 1st Printing), 1971, Vol. 3, p. 202-3. In 1962, in considering an immigration petition from a Jew who had converted to Christianity and become a monk, the Israeli Supreme Court ruled that "apostasy to Christianity removes that person from this nationality." For an account of the case, see <u>Encyclopedia Judaica</u>, *ibid.*, p.210.

19. A discussion of Vatican II's statements on the Jews can be found in Fisher's <u>Homework</u> and <u>Faith</u>. The text of <u>Nostra Aetate</u> and subsequent Catholic statements on relations to the Jews, as well as similar statements from the World Council of Churches and individual Protestant denominations, can be found in Helga Croner, <u>Stepping Stones to Further Jewish-Christian Relations: An Unabridged Collection of Christian Documents</u>, New York: Stimulus Books, 1977, and in Arthur Gilbert, <u>Homework for Jews: Preparing for Jewish-Christian Dialogue</u>, New York: National Conference of Christians and Jews (undated). Gilbert has an extensive discussion of recent changes in Christian churches.

20. <u>Nostra Aetate</u>, in Croner, *op. cit.*, p.2.

21. "The Christian Approach to the Jews," First Assembly of the World Council of Churches, Amsterdam, Holland, 1948, cited in Croner, *op. cit.*, p. 70.

22. Report of the Committee on the Church and the Jewish People to the Faith and Order Commission of the World Council of Churches, Geneva, Switzerland, 1968, cited in Croner, *op. cit.*, p. 78.

23. "Reflections and Suggestions for the Application of the Directives of *Nostra Aetate* (n.4)." Working Document prepared for the Holy See's Office for Catholic-Jewish Relations, by a special Commission. December 1969. Cited in Croner, *op. cit.*, p.7.

APPENDICES

APPENDIX 1

PROGRAM PLANNING WORKSHEET

Name of program..

Date scheduled...

Place..

Person in charge of program....................................

Phone number...

Other committee members..

....

....

Objectives of this program.....................................

Equipment needed in meeting area...............................

Furniture and room arrangement.................................

Audio-visual and other special equipment needed................

Refreshments to be served......................................

Order of meeting   Time Allotment

....

....

....

Describe the program that will take place......................

....

....

Announcements to be made.......................................

....

Anticipated costs:

Rental of equipment ....
Purchase of supplies ....

Fees to speakers ....

Cost of refreshments ....

Others ....
       ....

     PROJECTED TOTAL ....

Anticipated income:

Charge per participant (if any) ....

Anticipated number of participants ....

               Sub total ....

Other sources of income..

....

     PROJECTED TOTAL ....

TOTAL NET INCOME/EXPENSE...

Submitted by......................Date.............................

Approved by.......................Date.............................

Comments by supervisor...

....

....

APPENDIX 2

PROGRAM EVALUATION WORKSHEET

Name of program..

Date..Time..............

Place..

Weather..

Number of participants.......................................

Person in charge of program..................................

Names of those who actually worked on program.............

....

....

Was all needed equipment present and in working order?

....

Was room properly set up?....................................

Were refreshments served as planned?........................

Did the program go as planned?...............................

....

....

1. Did the program meet your objectives? ....

2. Did you consider it a success? ....

3. What factors do you think contributed to the success/failure of the program? ....

Actual costs:

....

....

Actual income:

....

Actual net income/expense ....

Compare this form with your original planning worksheet to see how you fared.

Submitted by ....Date ....

Comments by Supervisor ....

....

....

....

APPENDIX 3

PROGRAM EVALUATION FORM

Please answer as fully and honestly as you can. Your feedback is greatly appreciated and will be used in helping us to plan other programs.

1. The most interesting part of the program was:

2. I would have liked more of:

    Less of:

3. I have discussed these issues before: Yes_____ No_____

4. I would like to continue discussing the issues raised in the program:

    Yes_____No_____Indifferent_____

5. Interdating and intermarriage are not important issues for me at this point in my life:

    Yes_____ No_____Indifferent_____

6. Any suggestions for other types of programs on these topics:

7. Any additional comments that will help make future presentations better:

THANK YOU!

APPENDIX 4

WHAT IS OUTREACH?

Outreach is a program which aims to:

* Welcome those who seek to investigate Judaism;

* Welcome Jews-by-Choice as full citizens of the Jewish community;

* Welcome intermarried couples into the congregation. Outreach seeks to enable non-Jewish partners to explore, study and understand Judaism, thereby providing an atmosphere of support in which a comfortable relationship with Judaism can be fostered;

* Educate and sensitize the Jewish community to be receptive to new Jews-by-Choice and intermarried couples;

* Encourage people to make Jewish choices in their lives through community support, adult education and availability of Jewish resources;

* Assist young people in strengthening their Jewish identity and in examining the implications of interdating and intermarriage for themselves.

There is a national UAHC/CCAR Commission on Reform Jewish Outreach. Each UAHC Regional Office has an Outreach Coordinator on staff. In addition, many congregations have Outreach Committees.

WHAT IS THE HISTORY OF THE OUTREACH PROGRAM?

On December 2, 1978, Rabbi Alexander Schindler, President of the Union of American Hebrew Congregations, called upon the Board of Trustees to establish a program of Outreach which would develop responses to the needs of individuals converting to Judaism, intermarried couples, children of intermarriages and those interested in learning about Judaism. The UAHC Trustees unanimously adopted a resolution calling for the study and development of a program of Reform Jewish Outreach and endorsed the creation of a Joint Task Force with the Central Conference of American Rabbis. David Belin was named Chairman and Rabbi Max Shapiro Co-Chairman, followed by Rabbi Sheldon Zimmerman. This Task Force presented a report to the 1981 UAHC General Assembly, which then adopted five resolutions calling for a comprehensive program of Reform Jewish Outreach.

In 1983, the Task Force became a Joint UAHC/CCAR Commission on Reform Jewish Outreach with a mandate to develop programming, resources and materials for the various Outreach target populations. Lydia Kukoff was named Commission Director, David

Belin continued as Chairman, and Rabbi Steven Foster was named Co-Chairman. In 1988, Mel Merians was named Chairman, and Rabbi Leslie Gutterman was named Co-Chairman.

(For a detailed report of the Task Force, see "A Summary of the Report of the UAHC/CCAR Joint Task Force on Reform Jewish Outreach," August 1981.)

WHERE IS OUTREACH TODAY?

The program has expanded and currently includes programming for:

* Intermarried couples and couples contemplating intermarriage
* Children of intermarried couples
* Jews-by-Choice and those interested in choosing Judaism
* Parents of intermarried couples
* Inreach to born Jews on issues relating to Jewish identity and attitudes toward the changing Jewish community

The Outreach Staff currently includes an Associate Director, Rabbi Nina Mizrahi, as well as Sherri Alper, Consultant for Special Programming, and Outreach Coordinators in every UAHC region. Coordinators serve as resources for congregations in their region, working closely with professional staff and Outreach committees to design and implement a suitable Outreach program for each congregation. Coordinators also administer regional and sub-regional programs such as Introduction to Judaism, "Times and Seasons," and various follow-up programs for intermarried couples and Jews-by-Choice.

WHAT PROGRAMS DOES OUTREACH OFFER FOR INTERMARRIED COUPLES AND COUPLES CONTEMPLATING INTERMARRIAGE?

"Times and Seasons: A Jewish Perspective for Intermarried Couples" is a program which was created in response to the needs of the intermarried, to serve as the critical first step taken by unaffiliated intermarried couples seeking to explore differences in their backgrounds.

This eight-week discussion group is designed to clarify the Jewish partner's feelings about Judaism and to provide the non-Jewish partner with a broader understanding of Judaism and the Jewish community. The group facilitator is a trained professional. Relevant personal issues discussed include: religious involvement while growing up, the religious and cultural issues each partner confronts in the relationship with the other and with extended family, holiday celebrations, and each couple's concerns about the religious identity of their children.

Although the program is offered from a Jewish perspective, there is no attempt to convert the non-Jewish partner. The program, however, helps participants to articulate the differences between Judaism and Christianity. We believe that understanding these differences will allow fuller communication between partners and a more secure base for decision-making for the couple. Facilitators have been trained by the UAHC to lead these groups. A complete guide to the program, <u>Times and Seasons: A Jewish Perspective for Intermarried Couples - A Guide for Facilitators</u>, is available from the UAHC Press.

In addition to the "Times and Seasons" programs, many congregations offer a variety of programs for intermarried couples and their children. Sample programs are presented in <u>Reform Jewish Outreach: The Idea Book</u>.

WHAT PROGRAMS DOES OUTREACH OFFER FOR THE JEWISH PARENTS OF INTERMARRIED COUPLES?

Jewish parents of intermarried couples, or couples contemplating intermarriage, are one of the most accessible Outreach populations. Yet these parents often report feeling isolated within the very community that they have been a part of for so long.

The goals of the discussion groups for parents are:

* To provide participants with a non-judgmental, supportive setting in which they can meet with others sharing similar concerns;

* To provide participants with an opportunity to discuss the impact of their child's interfaith relationship on their family and to develop constructive responses to various family dilemmas that arise;

* To communicate the philosophy and objectives of Reform Jewish Outreach;

* To acquaint participants with existing Outreach programs in their own community;

* To provide participants with the clear message that the Reform Jewish community seeks to continue to reach out to them, their children and their grandchildren.

These groups are led by trained facilitators, many of whom have been trained at regional training sessions. A complete guide to the program, <u>Jewish Parents of Intermarried Couples: A Guide for Facilitators</u>, is available from the UAHC Press.

WHAT PROGRAMS DOES OUTREACH OFFER FOR THOSE CONTEMPLATING CONVERSION TO JUDAISM AS WELL AS FOR THOSE WHO ARE INTERESTED IN LEARNING MORE ABOUT JUDAISM?

Introduction to Judaism classes are offered on both the community and congregational levels. The main focus of the 12-18 week class is basic Judaism, including holidays, life cycle events, history, theology and Hebrew. Students learn what it means to live a Jewish life and how to begin to practice Judaism. This program may include a psychosocial component which deals with the personal implications of choosing Judaism. Post-introduction programs and various workshops and discussion groups are also offered. One of our hopes is that participants in these groups will integrate fully into temple life and take advantage of the many educational, social and worship opportunities in their own temples.

Some congregations offer a series of programs designed to help the new Jew-by-Choice become integrated into the Jewish community.

These programs often include discussion groups, workshops, study sessions and <u>Shabbatonim</u>. Program ideas may be found in <u>The Idea Book</u>.

WHAT PROGRAM HAS OUTREACH CREATED TO ASSIST RELIGIOUS SCHOOL TEACHERS, CANTORS, AND RABBIS IN DEVELOPING A SENSITIVITY TO THE NEEDS OF CHILDREN WHO HAVE NON-JEWISH RELATIVES?

The William and Frances Schuster <u>Guidelines for Outreach Education</u> reflect the cooperative effort of the UAHC Department for Religious Education and the Joint Commission on Outreach. The <u>Guidelines</u> contain three basic sections:

1) A statement of background and goals;

2) A faculty workshop to:

 * Provide background information about Reform Jewish Outreach,

 * Articulate some of the needs of children who have non-Jewish relatives,

 * Through values clarification exercises, help congregational and professional leadership clarify their own feelings regarding Outreach-related issues and policies,

 * Explore scenarios and strategies for dealing with various related situations which arise in the classroom;

3) A suggested approach to dealing with Outreach-related issues through the religious school curriculum.

Currently, the regional Outreach staff and the Department for Religious Education staff are available to assist with the faculty workshop. Training relating to classroom management and curriculum is handled by the Department for Religious Education, while the psychosocial component is handled by the Outreach staff.

WHAT PROGRAMS DOES OUTREACH OFFER FOR REFORM JEWISH YOUTH?

One of our goals is to assist young people in examining the implications of interdating and intermarriage for themselves as well as for the future of the Jewish people. We encourage our youth to explore and strengthen their Jewish identity.

A number of programs have been created for use in a variety of settings. Several of them are highlighted in The Idea Book and this publication.

HOW DOES OUTREACH PREPARE CLERGY, EDUCATORS, MENTAL HEALTH PROFESSIONALS AND LAY LEADERS TO WORK WITH THE VARIOUS OUTREACH POPULATIONS?

Facilitator training sessions for "Times and Seasons" and groups for the Jewish parents of intermarried couples are held on a regional basis. During the past few years, professional development courses have been offered through HUC-JIR to prepare clergy for meeting the changing needs of the Jewish community. HUC-JIR students also participate in special one-day Outreach seminars. An intensive one-week Outreach internship, hosted by Temple Emanuel in Denver, Colorado, provides students with an opportunity to experience and learn about the implementation of Outreach programs on a congregational level.

The Commission on Outreach offers on a regular basis workshops and presentations at various professional conferences, e.g. Central Conference of American Rabbis (CCAR), American Conference of Cantors (ACC), Coalition for the Advancement of Jewish Education (CAJE), and the American Psychological Association (APA). We also work closely with the CCAR Committee on Gerut.

HOW IS OUTREACH INVOLVED IN INREACH?

The ultimate goal of the Outreach program is to strengthen Judaism by helping individuals build their personal connectedness to Reform Judaism. We seek to assist born Jews and Jews-by-Choice in developing and enhancing their Jewish identity. The success of Outreach is dependent upon our ability to strengthen the bonds between members of the Jewish community and those who have chosen to associate with the community. These bonds are strengthened when every individual has a clear sense of his or her religious and ethnic identity. Outreach is not only about conversion and intermarriage. It is about being Jewish. Outreach enables us to look inward at who we are as Reform Jews and outward toward our changing community. Awareness of each enriches the other. A valuable resource which enables congregations to explore the relationship between Outreach and Inreach is Outreach and the Changing Reform Jewish Community: Creating An Agenda for Our Future - A Program Guide (available from the UAHC Press.)

APPENDIX 5

SUGGESTED READING

UAHC OUTREACH PUBLICATIONS

Program Guides:

<u>Introduction to Judaism: A Course Outline and Student's Resource Book</u>, compiled and edited by Stephen J. Einstein and Lydia Kukoff (Instructor's Guide also available)

<u>Jewish Parents of Intermarried Couples: A Guide for Facilitators</u>

<u>Outreach and the Changing Reform Jewish Community: Creating an Agenda for Our Future</u>

<u>Reform Jewish Outreach: The Idea Book</u>

<u>Times and Seasons: A Jewish Perspective for Intermarried Couples -A Guide for Facilitators</u>

<u>To See the World Through Jewish Eyes: Guidelines for Outreach Education: Developing Sensitivity to the Needs of Children Who Have Non-Jewish Relatives</u> (A volume of the UAHC William and Frances Schuster Curriculum)

Books:

<u>Every Person's Guide to Judaism</u> by Stephen J. Einstein and Lydia Kukoff

<u>The Jewish Home: A Guide for Jewish Living</u> by Daniel B. Syme

<u>Jews and Non-Jews: Getting Married</u> by Sanford Seltzer

<u>New Jews: The Dynamics of Conversion</u> by Steven Huberman

<u>Why Choose Judaism: New Dimensions of Jewish Outreach</u> by David Belin

<u>Your Jewish Lexicon</u> by Edith Samuel

Note: All of the above program guides and books are available through the UAHC Press, 838 Fifth Avenue, New York, NY 10021, (212)249-0100.

Films:

Choosing Judaism: Some Personal Perspectives (A Video Cassette) with Lydia Kukoff (Available in VHS or Beta format, $35, including video guide. To order, contact the UAHC TV and Film Institute, 838 Fifth Avenue, New York, NY 10021)

Intermarriage: When Love Meets Tradition Produced by Lydia Kukoff; directed by Ilana Bar-Din (Available in both 16mm and 1/2" VHS at special low rates to UAHC member congregations. Order films directly from: Direct Cinema Ltd., P.O. Box 69799, Los Angeles, CA 90069, or call (213) 652-8000. Make check payable to Direct Cinema Ltd. Contact your regional OUtreach Coordinator if you need further assistance. An in-depth discussion guide is available for $2.00. Oder guide from the National Outreach Office, UAHC, 838 Fifth Avenue, New York, NY 10021. Make checks payable to Outreach.)

ADDITIONAL PUBLICATIONS

A Guide to Interfaith Marriage: But How Will You Raise Your Children? Steven Carr Reuben. Pocket Books, NY, 1987.

The Intermarriage Handbook: A Guide for Jews and Christians. Judy Petsonk and Jim Remsen. Arbor House/William Morrow, NY, 1988.

Mixed Blessings: Marriage Between Jews and Christians. Paul and Rachel Cowan. Doubleday, NY, 1987.

122 Clues for Jews Whose Children Intermarry. Sidney and Betty Jacobs. Jacobs Ladder Publications, Culver City, CA, 1988.

Clues about Jews for People Who Aren't. Sidney and Betty Jacobs. Jacobs Ladder Publications, Culver City, CA, 1985.

The Jewish Experiential Handbook: The Quest for Jewish Identity. Bernard Reisman. Ktav, NY, 1979.

APPENDIX 6

REGIONAL OUTREACH STAFF

Canadian Council
Jessie Caryll
CCLC
534 Lawrence Ave. W.
Suite 213
Toronto, Ontario
Canada M6A 1A2
(416) 787-9838

Great Lakes Council/Chicago Federation
Mimi Dunitz
UAHC
100 W. Monroe St.
Chicago, IL 60603
(312) 782-1477

Mid-Atlantic Council
Elizabeth (Robin) Farquhar
61 G Street SW
Washington, D.C. 20024
(202) 488-7429

Midwest Council
Marsha Luhrs
UAHC
10425 Old Olive Street Road
Suite 205
St. Louis, MO 63141
(314) 997-7566

New Jersey/West Hudson Valley Council
Kathryn Kahn
UAHC
1 Kalisa Way
Suite 104
Paramus, NJ 07652
(201) 599-0080

New York Federation of Reform Synagogues
Ellyn Geller
UAHC
838 Fifth Avenue
New York, NY 10021
(212) 249-0100

Northeast Council
Paula Brody
UAHC
1330 Beacon St.
Suite 355
Brookline, MA 02146
(617) 277-1655

Northeast Lakes Council
Nancy Gad-Harf
6361 Timberwood South
West Bloomfield, MI 48322
(313) 788-0827

Northern California Council
Pacific Northwest Council
Lisa Cohen Bennett
UAHC
703 Market St.
Suite 1300
San Francisco, CA 94103
(415) 392-7080

Pacific Southwest Council
Arlene Chernow
UAHC
6300 Wilshire Blvd.
Suite 1475
Los Angeles, CA 90048
(213) 653-9962

Pennsylvania Council/
Philadelphia Federation
Linda Steigman
UAHC
2111 Architects Building
117 S. 17th St.
Philadelphia, PA 19103
(215) 563-8183

Southeast Council/
South Florida Federation
Rabbi Rachel Hertzman
UAHC
Doral Executive Office Park
3785 N. W. 82nd Avenue
Suite 210
Miami, FL 33166
(305) 592-4792

Southwest Council
Debby Stein
12700 Hillcrest Road
Suite 180
Dallas, TX 75230
(214) 960-6641

Director
Lydia Kukoff
UAHC
6300 Wilshire Blvd.
Suite 1475
Los Angeles, CA 90048
(213) 653-9962

Consultant for Special Programs
Sherri Alper
1684 Kenmare Drive
Dresher, PA 19025
(215) 628-4337

Associate Director
Rabbi Nina Mizrahi
UAHC
838 Fifth Avenue
New York, NY 10021
(212) 249-0100

National Coordinator of Programs
Task Force on the Unaffiliated
Dru Greenwood
UAHC
838 Fifth Avenue
New York, NY 10021
(212) 249-0100

NOTES

NOTES

NOTES

NOTES